J.E.M. Cowden.
April 1954.

THE ENIGMA OF THE HEREAFTER

THE ENIGMA
OF THE HEREAFTER

— The Re-incarnation of Souls —

By
PAUL SIWEK, Ph.D., D.D., D.ès Lettres

❖

PHILOSOPHICAL LIBRARY
New York

PRINTED IN THE UNITED STATES OF AMERICA

TABLE OF CONTENTS

PREFACE

Some years ago, I was invited to speak at the Philosophical Congress in Posen on the moral value of the theory of reincarnation of spirits. In several public lectures given later in Rome, Milan and Rio de Janeiro, I examined the same theory also from the religious and psychological point of view. Some of these lectures were published in French, Polish, Spanish and Portuguese.

The very kind reception which they found everywhere, the importance of the subject treated in them, and finally the urgent requests of distinguished friends, have determined me to write the present book, the result of my studies on this theory.

In order that all persons interested in this problem—emphatically called "the great problem of our epoch" by the Theosophists, Anthroposophists, Occultists, Neo-Buddhists, some liberal Christians, and a great branch of Spiritualism, (who all make it the fundamental truth of their beliefs) should well understand my ideas, I have endeavored to present them in the simplest manner possible, without, however, sacrificing anything of the truth to form.

INTRODUCTION

THE THEORY OF RE-INCARNATION
THROUGH THE AGES

1. The immortality of the soul belongs to that class of truths which constitutes the most precious heritage of humanity. Indeed, all people known to History hold by unanimous consent the conviction that the death of man does not entail extinction of the soul, and that the latter survives its severance from the body. This belief may be gathered from the monuments left us by antiquity: inscriptions, books dealing with theology, and funeral rites among primitive peoples, their philosophical systems, etc.

If we consider first ancient Egypt, we find there the celebrated "Book of the Dead", one of the oldest testimonies which has come down to us. That book is really nothing more than a vade mecum for the soul which leaves life on earth to enter Hades; it describes what the soul may expect and what it ought to do there; it indicates the chants to be sung, the prayers to be recited and the incantations to be spoken.

The Assyrian-Babylonians have left us a poem on the descent of the goddess Isztar to the Lower Regions. It tells the story of the soul after death, its sojourn in the underground world ruled by the God Nergal, and by the Goddess Eriszkigal who holds sway over "the great land" (this being the expression used in the poem for the underground world). Dense darkness prevails everywhere; the place is also called the "House of Darkness". The conditions in which the shades have to exist there are not at all enviable, for the soul that enters this place is surrounded by a sevenfold wall which makes it impossible for it to return to the outside world. Only very few individuals—and then only after a long delay

—will be allowed some day to leave and to resume their existence in less difficult conditions.

According to the Sacred Books of the Tribes of Iran (Medes, Persians, Parthians, etc.), books known under the generic title of the "Avesta",—the souls of the deceased are brought before the tribunal of the Gods, Mithra, Rashnu, Szaosha; their merits and trespasses are carefully weighed on a balance; after which the souls are led into a place of delight or else doomed to everlasting torture. As to the ancient Semites, Greeks, Romans, Celts, Germans, Slavs, etc., their belief in the life hereafter is so well-known that there is no need to dwell on it.

2. But how are we to conceive of human life devoid of any bodily substratum, the life of the soul alone? This is the problem which could not fail to confront the primitive mind. And we must admit that this problem was of a puzzling nature. Truly, life as experience manifests it to be, is based on matter; it depends on the body; is it not by means of the body connected with the soul that we get into contact with the world? Our first acquaintance with the world is due to our senses, our first reactions to the outside world are in the form of affections, emotions and other tendencies. Now, can the sensations and affections be conceived of as being independent of matter? How are we to imagine the life of the soul alone, a life devoid of any material support? That is the first difficulty which confronted primitive man.

But there is another difficulty. It is after death that the righteous expect to receive their full reward; and it is likewise after death that punishment will be meted out to the wicked. Now, how is it conceivable that man will enjoy real happiness if he is deprived of one of his essential parts, namely his body? On the other hand, how are we to interpret the meaning of punishment for a man who, having no body, cannot be affected by fire or frost, nor be subject to hunger or thirst?

These difficulties must have assumed a particular importance in the eyes of primitive man whose mentality was very much akin to that of a child. Like a child, primitive man does not easily grasp the intensity of mental life, its innermost joys, its silent sufferings; in his case joys and pains manifest themselves spontaneously in the noisy forms of cries, tears and spasms. The disciple of the Avesta dreams of his paradise in radiant light and the brightest colors, with the choicest tapestries woven of the most precious material. For Homer, happiness in the next world consists of the sojourn "in the Elysian Fields situated at the earth's limits" "where the sweetest life is enjoyed by human beings, where there is no snow, no severe winters, no rain, only gentle breezes rising from the Ocean to cool and refresh men"*. The religious ideas of other nations and their conceptions of happiness and punishment in the next world were not much loftier.

One understands the strong fascination that must have been exerted on so rude a mentality by the idea of re-incarnation, which did away in such a naive manner with the difficulties we have mentioned. In the place of the body buried in the ground, or reduced to ashes, the soul would be given a new body—human, animal or vegetable, no matter which; the essential being that the existence of man in another life might be conceivable, his happiness or punishment possible.

Let us further add that the doctrine of re-incarnation gave the mind of primitive man a satisfactory explanation of the phenomena of "heredity" which could not have failed to attract his attention from the earliest times; while it also helped to explain to him the "resemblances" between a departed spirit and a new-born child; lastly, re-incarnation seemed to justify the undeniable fact of some "analogies" existing between certain classes of persons and certain kinds of animals from the viewpoint of customs, passions, etc.

Those are the reasons—at least the principal ones—which must have influenced primitive thought in favor of the ideas of re-incarnation. They are the real origin of the success of this theory which Plotinus does not hesitate to call "a Faith universally professed".

3. However, we must not exaggerate. The doctrine of re-incarnation never attained a degree of universality comparable to that which characterises the doctrine of the immortality of the soul. Indeed, numerous peoples have always been opposed to the idea of re-incarnation. Others adopted it only very late, and it does not form a part of their primitive "Credo". For instance, we find no trace whatever of re-incarnation among the Persians; nor has the primitive religion of China any trace of it; it makes its appearance there only at a late date— through the influence of Buddhism. The idea of re-incarnation is equally foreign to the religion of ancient Egypt.

In order to refute my assertion, one might mention first the scene depicted on the sepulcher of Ramses III and on the sarcophagus of Sethos, where one sees a soul condemned to take the form of a pig. But no valid argument can be drawn from this in support of a general belief in re-incarnation among the ancient Egyptians; very likely this is one of the ways they imagined sinners were punished in hell. As to the "Book of the Dead" it simply describes the rules of Metamorphosis which enable the soul to assume at will the shape of any kind of animal; nay, even that of the body which it had discarded at the moment of death.

To understand how it is that the Greek historians and writers, Herodotus, Plato, Theophrastus and Plutarch, could assert that the Egyptians professed the doctrine of re-incarnation we must suppose that this doctrine had been thoroughly introduced into the Egyptian Credo, but at a much more recent date, through the influence of the Hindu religion.

An analogous peculiarity occurred in the Hindu religion itself. The idea of re-incarnation, wholly foreign to the religious literature of India during its oldest period, appears for the first time in the work entitled: "Satapatha Brahmana" or the "Brahman of the hundred ways"; that is during the second period of Hindu religious literature. And even then it makes its appearance completely transformed by the dogma which attributes to sacrifices the power of freeing the soul, once and for all, from the necessity of eternal migration through earthly existences[1]. This dogma, we easily see, does not agree with the Karma which proclaims the inexorable law of Justice; each individual must expiate himself his misdeeds; vicarious atonement—Redemption—is absolutely excluded.

The sacred books of the Jews sometimes mention the practice of the evocation of spirits[2]. But this has nothing to do with re-incarnation. Only the Cabala is an exception; its books Zohan (The Book of Splendour), Zohar-Hadash, Tiqqunim, state the doctrine of re-incarnation which forms an integral part of the mystic esoterism of the Cabala. But it is worth noticing that re-incarnation appears here as a fragmentary episode, without any intimate connection with the rest of the philosophical system of the Cabala; in fact, this doctrine stands in flagrant contradiction to the fundamental dogmas of the Jewish Religion admitted by the Cabala. The ecclesiastical authorities never sanctioned it, for in their view, re-incarnation was an infiltration of paganism (Egyptian and Hindu) through Manicheism and Gnosticism[3].

The doctrine of re-incarnation was wholly unknown to Greece when this country came into existence. It was only about the year 543 B.C. that a certain Terecides—a teacher of Pythagoras, it is said—introduced it. But it is Pythagoras himself[4] who is usually thought to have been the one who really introduced into Greece the theory of re-incarnation. It was later widely spread by Empedocles, the disciple of Pythagoras. It constitutes on the other hand the doctrinal basis of the cult of Dionysus, of the orphic hymns, and of the fantastic myth of the mysterious wheel of Fortune[5].

The theory of re-incarnation in Greece really owes its scientific form to Plato, who to explain and defend it uses treasures of fine psychological observation, of poetry and art, as we shall see later. But it is difficult to determine exactly how far the beautiful imagery used by the great philosopher and poet corresponds to his own convictions. What is certain is that he should not be taken literally[6]. In any case, Plato has avoided all those oddities which characterise the theory of re-incarnation as stated by his disciples, especially by Plotinus[7].

With reference to the Western World, we find the belief in re-incarnation to be particularly strong among the Teutons; it was from that belief that they derived their martial bravery, Appianus tells us[8]. The same belief is characteristic of the religious tenets of the Celtic peoples: the Greek historian, Alexander Polistorius, considered the Gauls to be followers of Pythagoras; in his opinion it was the expectation of future re-incarnation that caused them to despise death in battle[9]. In the pagan legends of Ireland, we find some points of resemblance with Pythagoras' ideas of re-incarnation. And lastly, several savage tribes of the West Indies also profess faith in re-incarnation.

4. With the advent of Christianity, the theory of re-incarnation begins to lose ground. For it is too much opposed to the spirit of the teaching of Christ, as we shall see later. Incessantly opposed by the Fathers of the Church and by ecclesiastical writers the doctrine soon disappeared from the western world. The efforts of the defenders of Christianity were greatly facilitated by the fact that the theory of re-incarnation had never met with a welcome reception by the Romans. Some poets—Horace[10], Virgil[11], Ovid—make allusion to the theory, but no Latin writer has given a serious thought to the matter. It was only after long intervals that certain heretics, the Albigenses and the Cathari recalled it from oblivion; but at each of its reappearances the theory suffered the same fate as the Manichean and Gnostic ideas to which it was closely related.

When in the XVI century Platonism became again, so to speak, the pole of philosophical thought, the idea of re-incarnation reappeared. Giordano Bruno and Campanella defend it eagerly. Later on Henry More, Lessing, Hume, and several poets of the romantic period became apostles of the theory. But it remained limited to a very small circle and had no influence on the spiritual life of the time.

5. Since the beginning of this century the idea of re-incarnation has captivated many minds. Here are the words which Irving Cooper, the founder of the Liberal Church in England, writes on the subject: We may notice almost with astonishment how rapidly and with what eagerness the cultured circles of our modern societies have taken interest in the idea of re-incarnation. Forty years ago, about a hundred persons took the matter up in a more or less superficial way, and those who adopted the idea as a basis of their philosophy were far fewer. Today there are in the west about a million people who have found in the idea of re-incarnation the most logical response to a great number of problems of a religious, philosophic and social order. Many of those who study the movement of contemporary thought believe that the idea of re-incarnation will soon be adopted by the majority of thinkers. No doubt it will be the great idea of our century, just as evolution was of the last century[12].

Theosophy, Anthroposophy, the Spiritism of the school of Allan Kardec, the Occultism of Papus, Messianism, etc. are now promoting with extraordinary vigor the spread of the doctrine of re-incarnation.

It must be noted though that this idea of re-incarnation which they defend should not be confused with that of simple "metempsychosis", professed by several ancient religions, and which is still to be met with among certain tribes. On the contrary, the modern disciples of re-incarnation consider "metempsychosis" as quite out-of-date and contrary to the idea of progress implied by Evolution, which forms the common basis of all modern theories of the life of the spirit. There is not—they say—a definite fall of the spirit. There are only pauses, or partial, temporary falls. To atone for them, the soul may be sometimes sentenced to descend to the lowest level of human life; it may well be banished to a world inferior to ours[13]. But it can never be degraded to a purely animal or vegetable life[14]. For by descending into the body of an animal, or of a plant, the soul would ipso facto lose the consciousness of its own personality, and therefore also the possibility of atoning for its misdeeds and deserving a new re-birth. This would be contrary to the law of Evolution.

*_The Odyssey_, p. IV, 562-568.

[1] See my book, _Em busca de Deus_ (_Looking for God_), Sao Paulo, 1944, 6, 72-77.

[2] _Levit._ XX, 6, 27; XIX 31. Deuteron. XVIII, 9, 10, 11, 12; I Reg. XXVIII, 3; IV Reg. XXI, 6.

[3] The Samaritans believed that the soul of Adam had been successively re-incarnated in Seth, in Hoah, in Abraham and in Moses.

[4] Not only popular tradition, but also the learned Greeks considered Pythagoras as the one who really introduced the theory of re-incarnation in Greece. CF. Aristotle, _De Anima_, I, 3, 407 b 22. According to the teaching of Pythagoras, animals possess a soul similar to ours. They only lack the organs needed to manifest their higher psychical life; the human soul may also be embodied in plants.

[5] Every time the wheel of Fortune completes a full revolution, all the changes in the world repeat themselves in the selfsame order in which they occurred previously.

[6] Cf. _Phaedon_ 114 C, D; _Phedrus_ 249 B; _Republ._ 617 D, 620 D.

[7] Just as the Cabalists, Plotinus liked to emphasize the law of retaliation (_lex talionis_): he who makes a bad use of wealth, will be poor in the next re-incarnation.

[8] _Rom. Hist._ IV: _De rebus Gallicis_, 3.

[9] C. J. Caesar, _De Bello Gallico_, lib. IV, c. 14.

[10] _Pers._ VI, 10.

[11] _En._ VI, 748-751.

[12] _Re-incarnation, the hope of the world_, Krotona, Introduction.—This is the message of hope that Theosophy brings to the Western World, a message of universal redemption from ignorance and hence universal emancipation from misery. The first fruits are appearing everywhere and the day will come when everybody will be ripe for the harvest and will fulfill the task which Logos has prescribed when giving you life (Annie Besant, _The ancient wisdom_, Adyar, 1939, pp. 253-254.)

[13] See Jerome A. Anderson, _Re-incarnation, a study of the human soul_, 1896, p. 66, 83-84.—_Karma_, 1896, p. 47.

[14] "Generally speaking, each new incarnation brings the person back to a slightly higher social level and amid better surroundings" (Irving S. Cooper, _Re-incarnation, the hope of the world_, Krotona, 1920, p. 43—William Q. Judge, _The Ocean of Theosophy_, Los Angeles, 1915, pp. 67-69.)

PART I

THE RE-INCARNATION OF SPIRITS AND RELIGION

Chapter I

BUDDHISM

1. If we ask a Hindu to explain why he holds so firmly to the belief in the re-incarnation of spirits he may simply reply: It is because our Faith so ordains it[1]; re-incarnation is one of our religious dogmas taught us by a venerable and immemorial tradition; our Sacred Books speak of it on almost every page; "Just as spring is re-born from winter," they say[2], "so life must be born again from death." "Just as a weaving-maid unravels a many-colored piece of cloth so as to renovate it and make it more beautiful," they add, "so likewise the soul leaves this body in order to put on a newer form"[3]. The Sacred Books have preserved a speech by Buddha who expounded to his disciples the doctrine of re-incarnation in the following terms[4]: "The re-incarnation of beings has its origin in eternity. It is impossible to find out the moment when beings until then immersed in ignorance and suddenly seized by the wish to live, commenced to wander higher and thither through interminable migrations. Which do you think exists in greater quantity: the water contained in the four oceans, or the tears that you have shed . . . when wandering here and there in the course of a long voyage, in the course of continual migrations, moaning and weeping, when you met what you hated, or that you did not find what you loved . . .? The death of your mother, the death of your father, the death of your brother, the death of your sister, the loss of your parents, the loss of your goods —all that you have experienced in the course of the ages". "It happens, oh! my disciples, that a monk full of faith, righteousness, knowledge, renunciation and wisdom thinks thus: Ah, if I could, immediately after my death, when my

[1]

body is beginning to decompose, know the happiness of being reborn in the house of a powerful prince. He broods over these thoughts incessantly, he occupies himself with them, they are his nurture. And, the desires . . . which he cherishes and thus cultivates will cause him to be actually reborn under similar conditions"[5].

In these texts—and we could easily lengthen the list (of them) indefinitely—the dogma of re-incarnation is clearly formulated. That is why the Hindu—unless he were to forsake the path traced for him by Tradition and the Sacred Scriptures—cannot deny re-incarnation. This doctrine forms an integral part of his Credo.

2. It is not contrary to the scientific spirit to admit something through faith in the testimony of others. We have already spoken of this elsewhere. That is why to reject the doctrine of re-incarnation solely because it is based on Faith, as is being done by several modern critics, is absolutely inadmissible. To have the right of rejecting it, we must show first that Faith in this particular instance is "illegitimate". And that will be shown by proving that it is "blind faith" in the wrong sense of the word, that is to say, a conclusion for which there are no means of finding the respective premises.

Of course, Faith is not knowledge. In the case of knowledge the premises are reached in a direct way, either immediately as with "veritates per se notae", or mediately by means of deductions. In the case of Faith the premises are not reached in this way. However, they have to be reached in some manner. They must be reached indirectly, that is to say, through the person who utters the truth which in this case stands for the conclusion. Thus, for instance, the Christian does not get the "mysteries" of his faith in a direct way but through Christ who reveals them to him. It is in this sense that Faith must always be founded on knowledge and end in knowledge. Otherwise it would only be a blind faith in the wrong sense of the word.

[2]

3. After this first remark we may be allowed to ask the question who in Buddhism has been able to grasp in a direct way the premises of the Faith in re-incarnation. Was it Buddha himself? But first of all the person of Buddha himself— so R. Grousset affirms—belongs rather to historical criticism than to history[6]. Now historical criticism has induced some eminent Orientalists, H. Kern, for instance, to consider Buddha a mythical person[7]. Others, it is true, do not go so far; they do not deny the historical existence of Buddha. However, his person seems to them so much deformed by legend that it becomes very difficult to know what is authentic in it[8]. Lastly, there are some Orientalists who uphold not only the historic existence of Buddha, but admit also, on principle, the possibility of reconstructing his personality; however, they hasten to add that looking at things from a purely historical viewpoint very few features which characterise the physiognomy of Buddha can be guaranteed[9]. The picture which tradition has left us of Buddha represents a type rather than a portrait, it shows indeed who were the first Buddhists, but it does not give the individual features which are the Buddha's own and belong to him only[10]; posterity has embellished the person of Buddha with a great number of narratives and fables ad maiorem Buddhae gloriam[11]. There is the first difficulty. We do not know exactly what Buddha taught about re-incarnation.

Here is another one. Supposing that re-incarnation, as professed by the Buddhists of our day, constitutes an authentic element of the doctrine coming from, or attributed to, Buddha, another point of great importance will still have to be settled, namely, whether it can be legitimately accepted as an act of religious faith. The life of Buddha, his way of acting, the tone he adopts in his teaching, all betray an over-excited temperament and greatly reduce the value of his testimony. It would be quite out of the question to try to go into his asceticism in connection with what we are dealing with just now; we do not in the least doubt his truthfulness, but merely the ontological value of his testimony. One may be pious, very pious, and at the same time be infected by different psychic troubles, be the dupe of illusions, or the victim of hallucinations. Illusions and hallucinations are pathological manifestations, just as "influenza" is, for instance. In order to eliminate their eventual presence, in the present case, we need some objective criteria, that is to say appropriate criteria for examination (carried on) from the outside, i.e. suitable for external observation.

Let us look then for these criteria. And for that purpose, let us first strive to answer the following question: What guarantee does Buddha give us that his doctrine is worthy of credit? So as to state our thoughts precisely, I take the liberty of making a digression. In what way does Christ justify faith in His "Divine Mission"? He appeals to the "testimony of the Father"; "If I bear witness of myself, my witness is not true. There is another who beareth witness of me[12]; the works which the Father hath given me to finish, the same works that I do, bear witness of me, that the Father hath sent me",[13] "the Father himself, which hath sent me, hath borne witness of me"[14]. Now, how has God borne witness to Christ? Is it by means of language similar to ours, language composed of sentences, words and syllables? But, if so, how can we distinguish with certainty His own language from the language of simple creatures? Would this not necessitate a new Word guaranteeing us the authenticity of His former word? In consequence we are tied up in a processus in infinitum which does not explain anything. That cannot be. The language in which God bears witness to Jesus Christ must be very different from ours. It must be a language *sui generis,* transcendental, a language suitable for God alone. This language is miracles. Christ gives us clearly to understand this point in his Gospel. And it must also be admitted that it is a language easily recognized by "whoever has ears to hear" and "eyes to see". Indeed, a miracle cannot be compared with a mathematical proposition; it is a fact found in Nature and which is ascertained by the senses and the intelligence.

4. Let us now return to our subject. Would Buddha base re-incarnation on the testimony of God? No. He never did so and he would not have known how to do so. For a miracle is to a certain extent a rent made in the structure of Nature, an infringement of its laws. In order to effect such a breach a force capable of checking that of Nature, of acting in opposition to its laws, is most evidently needed. In short, a force is required which does not form part of Nature and which is not subject to its laws; it must be a force which is superior, or in other words, a super-natural, a transcendental force, which could only be derived from a God possessing personality. Now, we know that the religion of Buddha does not recognise such a God[15]. The gods whom he adores are almost as much subject to Nature as man is, although possessing an incomparably longer and happier life than that of men[16]; they are not eternal[17], they are not even immortal.

In this religion the laws of Nature are the laws of God Himself whose power is thus determined and circumscribed. In consequence of such dogmas, no rent of which we spoke just now is possible in Nature. "Buddhism—so Bergson says—which brought deliverance to men, considered that the gods themselves needed to be delivered. Hence, it treated men and gods as being of the same kind, subject to the same fatality"[18]. Buddhism, says R. Grousset, is a kind of positivism grafted on the most childish beliefs of humanity[19]. There are some Orientalists who maintain that the primitive Buddhism was not even religion, but an attitude of the soul, or an attempt to regard the problem of human destiny from a single viewpoint, the viewpoint of sentiment[20].

That is why Buddha never had the idea of presenting his doctrine of re-incarnation as "the word of God". He simply borrowed the idea from Brahmanism, as is also the case with several other ideas in his theology. And so true is this that if we consider Buddhism from the point of view of its historic origin, says R. Grousset, it is nothing else but Brahmanic heresy, a heterodox system derived from the same source as the Vedanta, the Sankhya and Yoga[21].

[1] We will not insist on the word "Faith". It has not the same meaning for us as for a Hindu. We shall see this better later on.

[2] *Brahmana.* Cf. H. Oldenberg, *Le Bouddha,* Paris, 1934, pp. 51, 57.

[3] *Ibid.* p. 51.

[4] *Samyattaka-Nikaya,* t. II, p. 179. Cf. H. Oldenberg, *op. cit.,* pp. 242, 243.

[5] *Sanharuppatti-Suttanta (Majjhima-Nikaya)* n. 120. (See Oldenberg, *op. cit.,* p. 281.)

[6] *Histoire de la philosophie orientale,* Paris, 1923, p. 170.

[7] Cf. René Grousset, *Histoire de l'Asie, II: L'Inde et la Chine,* Paris, 1922, p. 23. Note 2.—*Histoire de la philosophie orientale,* p. 170.

[8] For instance Senart (Cf. his *Essai sur la légende de Bouddha,* Paris, 1882. Cf. R. Grousset, *L'Histoire de l'Asie, II: L'Inde et la Chine,* p. 23).—"I have been able to prove not that the Buddha never existed, that he was a solar or meteorological entity, a duplicate of Indra or of Apollo, as it has been often said I did, but that an epic legend had very soon crystallized around his name, that this legend which had not been created for him, but which he had inherited . . . mystic by nature . . ." (Emile Senart, *Les Castes dans l'Inde,* Paris, 1927, pp. 3-4).

[9] H. Oldenberg, *Le Bouddha,* Paris, 1934, p. 158.

[10] *Ibid.,* p. 156.

[11] *Ibid.,* p. 216.

[12] *St. John,* V, 31-32.

[13] *St. John,* V, 36.

[14] *St. John,* V, 37.

[15] Cf. R. Grousset, l. c., Paris, 1922, p. 21.

[16] Cf. H. Oldenberg, *Le Bouddha,* Paris, 1934, p. 245.

[17] *Ibid.*

[18] *Les deux sources de la Morale et de la Religion,* ed. XIII, p. 237.

[19] *Histoire de la philosophie orientale,* Paris, 1923, p. 174.

[20] Cf. R. Grousset, *Histoire de la philosophie orientale,* p. 174.

[21] *Ibid.,* p. 168.

CHAPTER II

BRAHMANISM

1. What we have just ascertained places another problem
before us: how does Brahmanism justify its faith in re-incarnation? In order to solve this problem, it is sufficient to study
the genesis of this dogma in the Hindu religion. It is an
indisputable fact, says a celebrated orientalist (Oldenberg),
that the ancient religion which expresses itself in the Rig-
Veda hymns, has always remained completely alien to the
idea of transmigration and periodic alternation of death and
rebirth. When saying this, he does not mean, as he mentions
further on, that this religion has nothing to say concerning the
life of the dead. No. For in the kingdom of Yama, those
who have crossed the black road of death, enjoy everlasting
happiness; those who have acted badly during the present life
must expect in the future life, in hell, darkness and misery;
when a spirit has once entered the world of the blessed or the
world of eternal darkness, the fate of each is definitely
sealed[22]. It is only towards the end of the Vedic period that
the belief in transmigration definitely took root in India[23].
This belief manifests itself clearly in the Upanishad Hymns,
the oldest of which go back—as is well known—to the VIIth
and VIth century B.C.[24].

These findings are of great interest. They show that the
dogma of re-incarnation was quite unknown in the primitive
religion of the Hindus, and that it is a comparatively recent
acquisition.

2. To what factors should we ascribe this acquisition? The
opinions of the orientalists on the subject are very diverse.
According to some, considerations of a political order played
a decisive part; the dogma of re-incarnation is said to have

been introduced by the sacerdotal caste of the Brahmans to protect their privileges and hegemony. These priests, by appealing to their own previous re-incarnations, wanted to make their origin go back to an immemorial antiquity. Other Orientalists maintain that the dogma was transmitted to the poets of the Upanishad Hymns by some other people, not Aryan, against whose influence they had not been able to preserve their beliefs in their original purity[25]. If so, it would be on craftiness and lies, or on weakness that such faith in reincarnation was based.

But there are not wanting Orientalists of repute who, rather than fly to weak conjectures, prefer to hold to the plain ignoramus et ignorabimus.

We need not take sides in this controversy. It is enough for us to record the following fact: the origins of re-incarnation remain shrouded in utter darkness; nobody can say by whom, when, how, by what right, nor in whose name the idea of re-incarnation has been raised to a fundamental dogma of the Hindu religion. And the recognition of this fact has important consequences. It shows us clearly that re-incarnation is a faith without a rational basis, hence a blind faith in the disparaging sense of that expression; a simple superstition.

[22] H. Oldenberg, *op. cit.*, p. 46. Cf. also p. 32.

[23] R. Grousset, *op. cit.*, p. 48.

[24] R. Grousset, *op. cit.* p. 74; *Histoire de l'Asie, II, L'Inde et la Chine.* p. 10 (note 2). Metempsychosis, says Senart, is quite alien to the Hymns. When it first makes its appearance, more or less veiled, more or less explicit, in the oldest Upanishads, are we in the presence of the first groupings of a doctrine which is looking for and elaborating itself? Are we in the presence of a partial infiltration in the esoteric atmosphere of a belief which was already dominant abroad? (Emile Senart, *Les Castes dans l'Inde*, Paris, 1937, p. 8.)

[25] R. Grousset, *Histoire de la philosophie orientale*, p. 32.

THE RELIGION OF CHRIST

1. Several partisans of the Re-incarnation theory hold that this doctrine is founded on the same basis as the other Christian dogmas, that is to say, on the very teaching of Christ[1]. No doubt, remark some of these Re-incarnationists (desirous to pass themselves off as Christians), re-incarnation which would extend the process of purification eternally, would by so doing "practically suppress heaven and hell" and thus also "eternal salvation"[2]. Such a re-incarnation would undoubtedly be in contradiction with the Christian doctrine. But re-incarnation reduced to the modest part of "purgatory", remains in perfect conformity with Catholic dogma[3]. It is even its authentic expression.

2. Before entering into details of the examination of this assertion, let us note at once a highly significant fact. Christianity of the present day does not profess re-incarnation. To convince oneself of this there is no need to undertake extensive scientific research. It suffices to enter any Christian church whatever, to listen to a sermon, or else to open the most usual Catechism. No mention is made of re-incarnation. On the contrary, an earnest appeal is made to work for our own salvation in fear and trembling—so long as the sun shines above our heads, for the night will soon come when we shall not be able to do anything for our salvation. The reward one will receive on giving up one's daily work in the dusk of life will remain the same for eternity.

The uniqueness of life on this earth confers upon Christian Eschatology a particularly austere character. That memento mori which it never ceases to din into the ears of the faithful is like a kind of tocsin; it stimulates us, it urges us, so that we may have time ╹ "save" our souls. Arrival at the final end possesses for Christianity the character of a real "salvation" ("salus" in Latin, σωτηρία in Greek). Any delay, even the inmost insignificant, may have fatal consequences; the parable of the wise and foolish virgins illustrates this truth in a striking manner. Only one eternity, only one life, this is the basic idea of all Catholic Eschatology of our days.

3. However, believers in the doctrine of re-incarnation do not acquiesce in this. To be sure, one cannot deny, so they say, that contemporary ecclesiastics manifest some hostility to the theory of re-incarnation[4]. But how can such an attitude be justified? Certainly not by invoking the doctrine of Christ as taught by the Holy Scriptures and Sacred Tradition. It is rather a matter of considerations of a political-pedagogical order; the wish, for instance, to secure for religious teaching the needed authority and to guarantee for it that efficiency which was lacking in the preaching of re-incarnationists among the primitives. For here is the sermon of the re-incarnist preacher: whoever has committed a sin will try in vain to flee the anger of God for that will pursue him beyond the grave; instead of quiet enjoyment in Paradise, in Heaven, he will have to return to this "vale of tears" to undergo again the hard "test" of life; moreover, he will have to begin life again on this earth until he has definitely mended his ways. But the hearer of such a sermon will exclaim: "What agreeable, what marvellous punishment! What! to return to this life—so full of miseries, it is true—but dearly cherished and untiringly and eagerly wished for? Let us sin then, sin as much as we can, if that is the best way, if not the only one, to return continually to this earth". So that which in the intention of the preacher ought to have turned one away from sin, becomes a real inducement to it. The sanction of the Law invites the violation of the Law! It is a subversion of all Morality.

And the re-incarnationists add: Ecclesiastical authorities, alarmed by the idea that such a result of the preaching might be possible, declared: "No, you will not return to the earth". They have endeavored to drive into the thickest heads this other conviction: "Whoever has wasted his life on this earth will thereby have forfeited his eternal life. He will not be able to correct what he has spoiled".

And this is why, the re-incarnationists triumphantly conclude, Christian authorities have given up the dogma of re-incarnation. Their principal motive was merely the wish to allow us an increase of their authority over the barbarians, and to be able to make use of the powerful means of moralisation that the threat of eternal damnation which immediately follows death constitutes.[5]

4. This explanation stands in evident contradiction to the history of the Church. Indeed, when did the Church profess re-incarnation? Not in our day, at any rate: no reincarnationist would think of maintaining this. Was it in the Middle Ages? Not at that period either. And on this point the most enlightened among them agree with us. They confess that "they do not find re-incarnation mentioned in the works of S. Thomas"[6], nor, in general, among any authorized representatives of Christian Theology. It is only mentioned among certain apostates of the time or by authors whose minds are alien to theological thought[7].

But let us go farther. Let us see what we may find in favor of the theory of re-incarnation during the periods which preceded the Middle Ages.

In the writings of St. Gregory the Great we may look in vain for the slightest mention of re-incarnation. This is very significant. For it is well known how vast and extensive is the theological horizon of the Holy Doctor; every question of any importance is dealt with by him. Now, re-incarnation is passed over in complete silence in his works. Why? Probably because in his opinion the matter no longer presented any interest. But we must not anticipate.

The same may be said of St. Peter Chrysologus. Only in one of his sermons he remarks, in passing, that the words of Christ calling St. John the Baptist "Elias" should not be understood in the sense given them by believers in metempsychosis; St. John the Baptist is called Elias in the figurative sense of the word: the spirit which animated him, the power which he manifested in his sermons, were an exact replica of the spirit and power which Elias had[8]. But St. Peter Chrysologus nowhere takes any part in the details of a discussion of the re-incarnation theory.

St. John Damascene maintains absolute silence on the theory of re-incarnation. And this silence is very eloquent. For the point in question is the very work in which the Holy Doctor exposes ex professo the doctrine of the Catholic Church on the soul and attacks the millenarism of *Origen*[9].

The angels as well as men after death no longer have any power to do penance for their faults[10], he says in this work. "After death there is no longer any possibility of being converted, nor of doing penance", he repeats with insistence[11].

Other more ancient Fathers do treat, it is true, of re-incarnation. Is it in order to recommend it to the belief of the faithful? Let us look at some texts.

"It is only heretical perversity (haeretica perversitas)—says St. Augustine—that may detect an affirmation of re-incarnation in the words of Holy Scripture, attributing to St. John "the spirit" and "the power of Elias"[12]. Porphyry—says the same Holy Doctor elsewhere—does not admit that the human soul may pass into the body of an animal. He must be praised for that. However, it would have been better to have altogether renounced the theory of re-incarnation: "he was no doubt ashamed to believe that a mother might some day carry her son on her back if it so happened that she became re-incarnated in the body of a mule, but he was not ashamed to believe that the mother might be transformed into a young girl and marry her son . . . Oh, how far nobler is the belief which the Saints and the Angels taught, the belief which the Prophets, directed by the spirit of God, proclaim, the faith which the Apostles preached . . . faith, I say, according to which souls only return once into their bodies (at the moment of resurrection)"[13].

For St. Jerome the theory of re-incarnation is an invention "of stupid philosophers and of heretics"[14]. St. Ambrose affirms that re-incarnation stands in contradiction to the natural order of the world, and still more so with the supernatural order[15]. Lactantius, great apologist of Christianity, does not hesitate to include re-incarnation among the fables suited for children[16]; the serious man, even if he endeavors to refute it, should not let people think that he is taking this matter seriously[17]. This is what the Latin Fathers think of re-incarnation. Now let us hear the Greek Fathers.

5. St. Gregory of Nyssa asserts that "the fable"[18] of re-incarnation is a doctrine which is an insult to humanity[19] for it disparages the dignity of man. Re-incarnation—says St. Gregory of Nazianzen—is the dream of "stupid people"[20]. It is the theory of those who are less reasonable "than the fishes", which they are supposed to have been in a previous existence, asserts St. Basil the Great[21]. Of all these theories, this is the vilest, maintains St. John Chrysostom[22]; that is why Christianity was right "in utterly overthrowing it"[23], so much so that "its name is no longer known by most people"[24]. Re-incarnation is an "absurdity", adds St. Cyril, for if the union of the soul with the body is intended to punish the soul for its faults, the salvation of the soul would necessarily imply deliverance from the body; hence these disastrous consequences: with reference to dogma—resurrection would have to be rejected; and as for Morals—the righteous should be condemned to death rather than the wicked; the wicked should be treated with all manner of attention so that they may live as long as possible and may thus atone for their faults[25].

6. These few testimonies are quite sufficient to prove that the present hostility of the Church to the theory of re-incarnation is not the result of utilitarian after-thought of recent date, as the believers in this doctrine claim it to be,

but that it already manifested itself with great insistence as far back as the IVth century of our era. The exclusion from the Christian Credo of the dogma of re-incarnation, if that ever occurred, must therefore have been effected during the first centuries of the Church. Let us fathom this period so long gone by, let us ask the Fathers of the primitive Church what they knew about re-incarnation.

7. St. Justin who studied carefully not only the thought of his contemporaries, but also the works of the old philosophers, took great interest in the idea of re-incarnation because it characterized the doctrines of the epigones of Pythagoras and Plato. The results of these studies are collected in his Apology and in his Dialogue with the Jew Tryphon. Now these two works clearly condemn the doctrine of re-incarnation[26].

St. Irenaeus attacked the idea of re-incarnation in the name of Science and of the Christian Religion. In the name of Science he remarks that there remains in our memory no vestige of those supposed previous existences[27]; in the name of Religion he opposes the dogma of the resurrection of the body; our God is powerful enough to give each soul his own body[28].

Tertullian pursues the theory of re-incarnation with that eagerness which is characteristic of him. Pythagoras—he says —who is said to have so well remembered his previous existences is a crazy liar[29]. He claimed to have taken part in the war against Troy. How are we to explain then why he showed so little courage in the sequel? Did he not flee from the war as far as Italy? If he had been, as he asserts, Pyrrhus the fisher, in a previous life, how can we account for his aversion to fish? (It is known that he never ate any)[30]. And Empedocles? Did he not allege that he had been a fish in a previous life? That must have been the reason why he threw himself into the crater of a volcano: he wanted to be fried[31]! The migration of souls into the bodies of animals is so absurd a supposition that even heretics have never dared to defend it[32]. But re-incarnation, as some of them make it out to be, cannot be admitted either: it is opposed to the notion of the justice of God, which demands that punishment should be shared by the very body that committed the sin and by no other.[33] Their thesis does not agree with the dogma of resurrection that presupposes the return of the soul to the very body which it left at the time of death[34].

For Clement of Alexandria the doctrine of re-incarnation is an arbitrary theory, for it is not founded either on the suggestion of our consciousness[35] or on the Christian faith; the Church has never professed it, but only heretics, particularly Basilides and Marcion; Basilides inferred it from an erroneous interpretation of the passage of the Holy Scriptures where it is said that God punishes the sins of men up to the third and fourth generation[36].

The ideas of Origen on re-incarnation resemble at more than one point those of Clement of Alexandria. Basilides— he says—has inferred the idea of re-incarnation by mistaking the words of St. Paul: "I have lived in other times without law" . . . He did not notice that the expression "in other times" does not refer to a previous life of St. Paul's, but only to a previous period of his life on this earth. That is how he was misled into debasing "the apostolic doctrine" to the level of absurdities and profane fables[37].

Notwithstanding the text just mentioned, Origen is often taken to be a supporter of the theory of re-incarnation. What is quite remarkable is that St. Jerome shares this impression. According to him Origen is supposed to have really considered re-incarnation as a plausible hypothesis. Several authors suggest various solutions to this riddle: some of them believe that St. Jerome based his opinion on texts interpolated into the works of Origen; others think that Origen was once really favorably inclined towards this theory, but that he gave it up later on[38]. It seems to me that St. Jerome did not make a clear cut distinction between the "re-incarnation" of souls and their "pre-existence". Now, these are two very different things. By "pre-existence of the soul" only this is to be understood: before being united to their bodies souls have lived for some time without any union with matter; the moment of their union with the body does not coincide with that of their creation. The expression "pre-existence of souls" does not tell us whether the union of the soul with the body is to be effected only once or several times. On the other hand, re-incarnation of souls does not presuppose that they have been created before bodies, and that it is only after having spent some time without this body that they were joined to it. Hence there is an essential difference between the theory of re-incarnation of souls and that of their pre-existence. That is why certain thinkers have been able to profess the latter thesis without defending the former. In my opinion, Origen was a supporter of belief in the pre-existence of souls but not in their re-incarnation.

Minutius Felix maintains that the idea of re-incarnation is only a corruption of the dogma of the immortality of the soul. But if the idea of re-incarnation is further debased by the myth of the human soul transmigrating into the bodies of animals one really ceases to treat the question seriously[39].

Finally we reach St. Hippolytus; "Christians," he said, "do not expect the ἐνσωμάτωσις, re-incarnation, but the resurrection of their own bodies."[40] These words of the glorious martyr of the Christian Faith characterize the attitude of the primitive Church with reference to re-incarnation.

Whatever may be the opinion of Origen on the question we have just examined, the Christian doctrine of the first centuries of Christianity concerning re-incarnation remains perfectly clear. The voices of some authors, were they as powerful as that of Origen, would not be able to break the imposing harmony which the unanimous Credo of the primitive Church presents to us.

8. It is true that some Fathers whose testimonies were mentioned above, do refer to this kind of re-incarnation to which is, now-a-days, generally given the name of "metem-

psychosis", or in other words to that form of re-incarnation which consists in a migration of human souls into the bodies of animals. However, the fact that when refuting the thesis of metempsychosis, they never mention any other kind of re-incarnation (in accordance this time with Christian dogma) clearly reveals the nature of their intimate convictions concerning this problem; they do not know, nor do they want to know any re-incarnation of this kind. Their condemnation of re-incarnation assumes therefore an absolute character. It admits of no reserve, of no exception. Any kind of re-incarnation, whatever it may be, is opposed to Christian doctrine.

If we state lastly that certain Fathers receive their faith from direct disciples of the Apostles (for instance: St. Irenaeus from St. Polycarp) and that all, without any exception, wholeheartedly attached to Christian orthodoxy, never allowed the slightest alteration of their Credo, their testimony gains ipso facto a quite exceptional value; their voice is the voice of the Apostles; now the voice of the Apostles is the voice of Christ in person. The condemnation which they utter against the theory of re-incarnation is like a condemnation uttered by Christ himself.

[1] See A. Schopenhauer, *Le monde comme volonté et comme représentation*, traduit par A. Burdeau, t. III, ed. 7, chap. 47, p. 319.—Annie Besant, *Reincarnation, a Christian doctrine*, Chicago, Illinois, pp. 8-27.—William O. Judge, *The Ocean of Theosophy*, Los Angeles, 1915, pp. 63-64.

[2] W. Lutoslawski, *Preesistenza e Rincarnazione*. Torino, 1911, p. 7.

[3] *Ibid*. Let us note that Theosophists often compare certain states through which they assert that the soul passes with "purgatory". "Kameloka", A. Besant says, ". . . as has already been intimated, a part of the astral plane, not divided from it as a distinct locality, but separated off by the conditions of consciousness of the entities belonging to it" (*The ancient wisdom*, Adyar, 1939, p. 83). There are in it "human beings who have lost their physical bodies by the stroke of death, and have to undergo certain purifying changes before they can pass on to the happy and peaceful life" (*ibid.*, p. 83). "This region represents and includes the conditions described as existing in the various hells, purgatories, and intermediate states, one or other of which is alleged by all the great religions to be the temporary dwelling-place of man after he leaves the body and before he reaches heaven" (*ibid.* p. 83). "It does include conditions of suffering, temporary and purificatory in their nature, the working out of causes set going in his earth-life by the man who experiences them" (*ibid.*, p. 84).

[17]

THE ENIGMA OF THE HEREAFTER

4 See Annie Besant, *Reincarnation, a Christian doctrine*, Chicago, p. 22.
5 Prof. W. Lutoslawski, *Niesm. duszy*, III, pp. 298-99.
6 W. Lutoslawski, *Preesistenza e Rincarnazione, cd. cit.*, p. 8.
7 See e.g. Annie Besant, *Reincarnation, a Christian doctrine*, Chicago, Illinois, pp. 22-23. "The teaching of Reincarnation taught in the Early Church" (A. Besant, *Esoteric Christianity*, New York, 1902, p. 238).
8 *Sermo* 88; P. L. 52, 449.
9 *De fide orthodoxa*, lib. II, c. 1; P. G. 94, 864.
10 *De fide orthodoxa*, lib. II, c. 4; P. G. 94, 877.
11 *Dialogus contra Manichaeos*, n. 75; P. G. 94, 1573.
12 *In heptateuchum*, lib. IV, c. 18; P. L. 34, 725.
13 *De Civitate Dei*, lib. X, c. 30; P. L. 41, 310.
14 Lib. II, c. 11; P. L. 26, 74.
15 Lib. II, n. 130; P. L. 16, 1412.
16 *Divinarum Institutionum*, lib. III: *De falsa sapientia philosophorum*, c. 18; P. L. 6, 409-410.
17 *Divinarum Institutionum*, liv. VII: *De Vita beata*, c. 12, P. L. 6. 777.
18 *De hominis opificio*, c. 28; P. G. 44, 232.
19 *Ibid.*
20 *Carmen VIII: De Anima*, v. 32; P. G. 37, 449.
21 *Homilia VIII in Hexaemeron*, 2; P. G. 29, 167.
22 *In Joannem homilia* II al. I; P. G. 59, 31.
23 *Ibid.*
24 *Ibid.*
25 *In Joannis Evang. lib.* I, 17; P. G. 73, 142; lib. I. 23; P. G. 73, 144; lib. I. 6; P. G. 73, 135.
26 *Apologia I pro Christianis*, 61; P. G. 6, 420; *Dialogus cum Tryphone Judaeo*, 4; P. G. 6, 486.
27 *Contra Haereses*, lib. II, c. 33; P. G. 7, 830-831.
28 *Ibid.*, lib. II, c. 33; P. G. 7, 833.
29 *Liber de anima*, c. 28; P. L. 2, 740.
30 *Ibid.*, c. 31; P. L. 2, 744.
31 *Ibid.*, c. 32; P. L. 2, 745.
32 *Ibid.*, c. 34; P. L. 2, 751.
33 *Ibid.*, c. 35; P. L. 2, 710.
34 *De resurrectione carnis*, c. 1; P. L. 2, 841.
35 *Eclogae ex Scripturis Propheticis*, XVII; P. G. 9, 706.
36 *Excerpta ex scriptis Theodoti*, XXVIII: P. G. 9, 674; *Stromatum* lib. III, c. 3; P. G. 8, 1114-1115; lib. IV, c. 112; P. G. 8, 1290-1291.
37 *In epistolam ad Romanos*, lib. V; P. G. 14, 1015. Cf. also *In Evangelium Joannis*, P. G. 14, 220.
38 A. Bukowski, S. J., *La réincarnation selon les Pères de l'Eglise*, "Gregorianum", 1928, pp. 65-91; *L'opinion de Saint Augustin sur la réincarnation des âmes*, "Gregorianum", 1931, pp. 57-85.
39 *Octavius*, c. 34; P. L. 3, 361. Cf. also D. Nic. Le Nourry, *Dissertatio in Marci Minutii Felicis librum qui Octavius inscribitur*, P. L. 3, 476-477.
40 *Adversus Graecos* (fragment), 2, 47, Cf. D'Ales, *La théologie de Saint Hippolyte*, Paris, p. 194, note 2.

PART II

THE THEORY OF
RE-INCARNATION AND PSYCHOLOGY

CHAPTER I

PLATONISM AND THEOSOPHY

1. As early as the first centuries of our era, Saint Justin*, Tertullian**, Saint Irenaeus[1], Clement of Alexandria[2], Eneas Gazaeus[3], and St. Augustine[4] invoked against the thesis of re-incarnation the following fact: we retain no memory of our alleged former lives. How can this be explained? We remember our dreams when we have been sleeping only a short while, how could we forget all that we have lived through during long years? This difficulty is serious. In fact, we spontaneously retrace in our memory the most insignificant happenings of a youth left already far behind; by way of certain mnemonic methods we are able to revive memories which seemed buried forever; but whatever effort we may make, we never succeed in recalling the least detail of a former existence. The light of memory extends to childhood; then, it is night, a dark night with no shining star.

How can we explain this strange deficiency in one of our faculties? The believers in re-incarnation are perfectly conscious of the importance of this objection. One of them sincerely admits: "The most important argument against re-incarnation is the almost complete oblivion of past lives; memories of re-incarnation are extremely rare; this is why they may be considered as individual illusions . . . If it be true that we have already lived several lives, how can we explain not only the general oblivion of former lives but also the oblivion of their preceding lives in eminent minds, and especially in the Mystics, who have reached Being even to its essence"[5]? Another says: "It is not to be denied that this is the strongest objection to our doctrine"[6].

Diverse attempts have been made to set aside "this old difficulty", to use Mrs. Blavatsky's words[7]. We are going to test the most important of these attempts in succession.

[21]

2. Here is how Plato explains the general oblivion of our past lives: before being re-incarnated and starting a new existence, the souls drink the water of the Lethe; it is thanks to this draught that they forget their past and have the happy illusion of being born for the first time.

Saint Irenaeus did not have any difficulty in discovering the contradiction contained in this mythological explanation. "If the chalice of oblivion (oblivionis poculum) possesses the power of wiping out all memories, how do you now happen to know it? Before your soul entered your body, it was offered the chalice of oblivion! If, in spite of this . . . you are able to keep the memory of this chalice, . . . you ought to be able to recall as well other details of your past life"[8].

In order to give the platonic solution a more scientific character, Plato's partisans asserted that the "chalice of oblivion" mentioned above is no more than a symbol; that it represents the body which the soul assumes with each new re-incarnation and which, according to them, possesses the intrinsic virtue of depriving it instantly of all memories. But Saint Irenaeus answered them: if this were so, the body to which we are now bound should constantly wipe out whatever memories we may have. Experience proves the contrary since we hold in our memory a number of details of our daily life.

3. In spite of its intrinsic weakness, the platonic theory has survived to this day[9]. Only its form has undergone a change. The new presentation that Theosophy has given to the platonic thesis deserves notice.

According to the founder of the Theosophical Association, this is the way our body replaces in its functions the water of the river Lethe. First, says Mrs. Blavatsky, one should distinguish carefully between "memory" and "reminiscence" (remembrance, recollection). Memory is a function which, by means of association, reproduces in our consciousness the perceptions of the past; it might be called "fantasy"[10]. Memory depends entirely on the brain and its physiological con-ditions[11]; it is common to Man and animals[12]. Reminiscence, on the contrary, is a "perception of intuition" which has noth-ing in common with the "physical brain"; it is a function of our spiritual Ego; it contains all the visions usually called abnormal, beginning with the inspirations of genius and ending with the fancies of fever, or with insanity[13]. It is a "spiritual memory" which in no way depends on material conditions.

Therefore, asks Mrs. Blavatsky, why should we be sur-prised that we do not recall our past lives? With every one of our successive deaths, our Ego lays down its physical ele-ments like a worn out piece of clothing; with every one of our re-incarnations, it puts on new clothes[14]. Looking into our present organism for the memory of our past lives is as absurd as scrutinizing with a microscope a shirt which a criminal has never worn, in order to discover some trace of his crime[15]. Neither the "physical body", nor the "astral body" nor the "mental body",[16] which now are ours have anything in common with the physical body, the astral body, and the mental body, which in the course of our past incarna-tions, were the seat of our thoughts and our feelings. It is true. that, under the "corporal" clothes which we throw off with each re-incarnation, the same spiritual Ego always remains, indestructible, eternal. But the Ego is not wont to inscribe his intimate secrets on his clothes.

One must admit that this theory would explain fairly well the absence of memories of our past lives. It remains to be known on what scientific basis one might build it. In particular, how could it be proved: 1° that man is composed of several bodies (a physical body, an astral body, a mental body)? 2° that the mind of man from time to time leaves these bodies to live in other bodies? The theosophists answer: both our assertions are based upon "unquestionable facts, on facts proved"[17] by the "psychic sciences"[18].

[23]

Let us weigh these "facts" a little more carefully. Whoever is endowed with clairvoyance even to the slightest degree, says Irv. S. Cooper[19], can notice a thin "mist of luminous matter" around all living human bodies, at an approximate distance of eighteen inches. This mist is called "aura"[20]; it is oval in shape and its characteristic color may change under the influence of the feelings and thoughts of the person it is surrounding. During sleep, and at death, the aura leaves "the physical body"; it is then possible to study it in an isolated state. It has been found that in the midst of this oval and slightly luminous mist of the aura a kind of replica of the physical body appears, of the same size but of a much greater luminosity than that of the aura, since this kind of nucleus alone absorbs 99 hundredths of the matter of the cloud. Further research has demonstrated that this image of the Ego, (as well as the aura itself), consists of three bodies which interpenetrate and show colors and dimensions that are almost identical. These three bodies, indispensible instruments of human consciousness are: the body of feeling (astral body), the body of thought (mental body), and the body of soul (causal body). Acting in the heart of the emotional body (astral), our consciousness finds expression in feelings, affections, wishes, passions, any kind of emotion; acting in the mental body, it forms concepts, images, symbols, unites and associates them; this is concrete thought. Finally, within the limits of the causal body, it finds its expression, in abstract thoughts and superior feelings[21].

As long as the physical body is surrounded and penetrated by the mist of the aura, the brain responds to vibrations of the consciousness and reproduces them; and we can then say that the body is alive, that it possesses a soul. At the time of death this link is broken. We are then entitled to say that the soul has left the body.

After death, we retain consciousness and activity in that part of the invisible world which closely surrounds the earth, that is in the astral sphere. There we spend a few years, participating in the manifold and strange life of that sphere. The concept of this period corresponds to the Catholic idea of purgatory, according to Annie Besant[22]. There we slowly get rid of our inferior energies, our animal desires and those passions to which we may have been slaves during our earthly life[23].

When this astral body, which is the agent of our consciousness in that first period following death, has fulfilled its task, any relation with this period is also broken and is followed by a kind of astral death. Then an intense conscious life begins in another sphere of the invisible world called the mental sphere, which could be called heaven. It is the happiest period of the whole cycle; no shadows of suffering are there[24]. In this superior world the work of the assimilation of those personal experiences realized on earth is accomplished. Everything we have acquired during this life becomes capacities, innate virtues of our character[25].

After a while we leave that world also, leaving behind our luminous mental body, and we then succeed in knowing our own identity, our immortal Ego. However, its immediate agent, the "causal" body, develops through the centuries; the mental body, the astral and the physical change with each re-incarnation.

These are, in brief, the principal "facts" that, according to the theosophists, are sufficient to explain why we possess no precise memory of our former lives. But, are these "facts" based on experience as claimed by the disciples of re-incarnation? Have they ever been "scientifically ascertained"?

So far as the aura is concerned which, according to them, surrounds living beings, we do not want to dispute a priori the possibility of its existence. Like all matters brought to a temperature higher than that of their own sphere, the human body radiates, without ceasing, emanations that are still imperfectly known. In particular, vapors deriving from perspiration may reach an unusual volume[26]. Due to diverse excretions, the body is constantly surrounded by a special atmosphere, the odor, quantity and intensity of which are in direct proportion to the metabolism pertaining to each organism, to the nature of the food he uses, to such or such a disease of which he is a victim, etc. For instance, it is well known that a child emits the odor of butter (and this because the milk he drinks contains a certain quantity of butter); that the adolescent at the time of puberty has a smell which reminds one a little of a male goat; the diabetics are characterized by an odor of acetone; a person who relishes onions by an acrid and caustic odor, etc. In the same way, we are able to recognize a feverish state through the sense of smell. Let us add that the human body (like any other) constantly exudes all around it a considerable quantity of subtle particles that are scattered in the surrounding atmosphere and finally saturate it; the body certainly also emits electric fluids, not to mention radio-electric or radioactive emissions.

All these natural phenomena may contribute to create around the living being a kind of "aura". Although imperceptible under normal circumstances, the aura may sometimes be perceived by some one whose sensitive faculties, under the influence of diverse factors (somnambulism, hypnosis, hysteria, etc.) happen to be exceptionally acute. Consequently, on principle, (we insist again on this point), we do not entertain any prejudice against the existence of the aura. Our difficulty only begins when the question is to determine its nature.

In fact, by what method has one ever "ascertained" that the aura leaves the physical body? What instruments have been used to capture the replica of the ego in the midst of this aura? How could one scientifically verify that it really consists of three bodies occupying the same space? Has it been demonstrated that one of these really expresses the conscious states in the form of "feelings", another in the form of "concepts", and the last one in the form of "abstract thought"? By what means could the aura be separated from the body and examined individually? By what stratagem could these three elements be differentiated although they are about "the same color" and "interpenetrate each other"? Where and how did Mrs. Besant ascertain the existence of "the organ of the future", which perceives the phenomena of "the astral world", or that the pineal gland unites the brain to the mental world?[27] By what mathematical system was the number of years calculated which, after death, we spend in each of the different supra-terrestrial spheres? How was it possible to observe the intimate life of the ego in each one of these spheres, to watch it in its process of "purification", that is to say, during the transformation of experiments carried out on earth into "capacities" and "innate virtues"; during the very organization of that body which it is going to reclaim for a future life. How many riddles and mysteries there are which cannot be solved, for it is impossible to take seriously the testimony of "hypnotized" persons, of "mediums" or even of "initiates" and that for reasons which will be given a little further on.[28]

These riddles and mysteries become real contradictions as soon as we are told of the "vibrations of consciousness" or of a "vibratory relationship" which constitutes the union of body and soul. Abstract thought, concepts, feelings, can in no way be reduced to a "vibration". It is true that psychic facts express themselves through visible gestures, motions, changes in the color of the face, etc., which can be intercepted and retained on a stereotype-plate. However, neither the gesture, nor the motion, nor the change of color are, in themselves, thought or feeling. The theories of theosophists shock us by their excessive materialism, a materialism which they do not deny. According to Mrs. Blavatsky, spirit and matter are really one and the same thing, spirit is "potential matter" and matter is nothing but "crystallized spirit"[29].

Are these really "experimental facts" which demonstrated to the founder of the Theosophical Association that "spirit and matter" are one and the same thing? It is much more

[27]

probable that she was inspired by a "materialist philosophy"[30] like Haeckel's or Darwin's which she adopted without sufficient reflection.

Dialogus cum Tryphone Judaeo, 4; P. G. 6, 486.
Tertullian, *Liber de anima*, c. 31; P. L. 2, 702.
[1] *Contra Haereses*, II, 33; P. G. 7, 830-831.
[2] *Eclogae ex Scripturis prophetics*, XVII; P. G. 9, 706.
[3] P. G. 85, 902.
[4] St. Augustine, *Confess.*, lib., l.c. 6—see also *ibid.* lib. 10, c. 17.
[5] W. Lutoslawski, *Niesm. duszy*, ed. cit., pp. 287-288; *Prees. e Rincarnaz.* ed. cit., pp. 61, 62.
[6] L. Figuier, *Le lendemain de la mort*, Paris, 10 e ed., 1895, p. 341.
[7] *The Key to Theosophy*, Point Loma, Cal. 1913, p. 122. Annie Besant says: The main difficulty with many people is the reception of the doctrine of re-incarnation (*The ancient wisdom*, Adyar, 1939, p. 220). See Jerome A. Anderson; *Re-incarnation, a study of the human soul*, S. Francisco, 1896, p. 69: "the chief objections to re-incarnation". Papus, G.A.V. Encausse, *La réincarnation et la métempsychose*, Paris, 1912, p. 136.
[8] *Contra Haereses*, II, 33; P. G. 7, 831-832.
[9] "The inborn ideas" which we possess—Figuier says—are best explained by the supposition of re-incarnation (*Le lendemain de la mort*, 10 e ed. Paris, 1894. Chap. XVI, pp. 299-313). Man keeps from a former re-incarnation, vague memories, which we call inborn ideas, says Allan Kardec (*Le livre des Esprits*, Paris, livre II, ch IV, p. 94).
[10] *The Key to Theosophy*, Point Loma, 1913, p. 125.
[11] *Ibid.*, pp. 123, 124.
[12] *Ibid.*, p. 123.
[13] *Ibid.*, p. 124.
[14] *Ibid.*, p. 127.
[15] *The Key to Theosophy*, Point Loma, 1913, p. 127.
[16] Mrs. Blavatsky remarks that the different Oriental Schools indicate a different number for the principles of the "Ego" (*The Key to Theosophy*, Point Loma, Cal, 1913, VII, pp. 115-116). But the substance of their teaching remains the same (*ibid.*, p. 116). See also Annie Besant, *The ancient wisdom*, ed. cit., Chap. I-VI, pp. 45-170, 35-42.
[17] H. P. Blavatsky, *l. c.*, p. 86.
[18] H. P. Blavatsky, *l. c.*, p. 128, 106.
[19] Irving S. Cooper, *Re-incarnation the hope of the world*, Krotona, 1920, p. 31-35. Irving S. Cooper, *Theosophy simplified*, Kroton, 1919, Chap. III, pp. 27-34, Chap IV, 35-42. Annie Besant, *Man and his bodies*, Chicago, 1923, pp. 9-87.
[20] This word is taken from the alchemists of the Middle Ages and Paracelsus, says Annie Besant (*La vie occulte de l'homme*, pp. 42-43).
[21] See C. Jinarajadasa, *First principles of theosophy*, Adyar, 1922, Chapter VI, pp. 98-110.
[22] "The Roman Catholic names it Purgatory" (*Esoteric Christianity*, New York, 1902, p. 241).
[23] In the period of our life, says I. S. Cooper, we can keep in touch with our friends, whether they are still in their physical body, or already in the

"beyond". Mrs. Blavatsky says, on the contrary, that contact between the dead and the living is possible only during the few days which immediately follow the death of the individual and before the latter enters the devanic period. In this purgatory, writes J. C. Chatterji, one is allowed to sin at will by taking possession of the body of a spirit-medium (*La philosophie esotérique de l'Inde*, Bruxelles, 1898. p. 761).

24 The future rest, asserts Mrs. Blavatsky, consists in a blessed ignorance of all the miseries one has left behind (*The Key to Theosophy, ed. cit,*, pp. 145, 147).

25 See Annie Besant, *The ancient wisdom*, Adyar, 1939, pp. 143-151, 101-104. J. C. Chatterji, *La philosophie esotérique de l'Inde*, Bruxelles, 1898, pp. 78-79.

26 Normally, man exhales about half a litre of sweat a day. However, when his body is submitted to an exceptional temperature (due to physical toil in the sun, for instance, or to a steam bath) it may exude more than half a litre an hour.

27 Annie Besant, *The changing world*, Chicago, III., 1910, pp. 51, 53, 57-58, 125.

28 In reference to this Annie Besant quotes Kilner's experiences: by using different lights and shadows, he "showed to the physical eye of man" part of this invisible matter. Moreover, she adds, it is enough to press rather strongly the hand of a hypnotized person and to shake it violently as if one were angry, to communicate anger to this person, by means of the "astral manner".

From this first experiment one might, at the most, infer the existence of the aura, but not its composition. The second experiment is the classical fact of "suggestion", which is well known to psychology.

29 *The key to Theosophy, ed. cit.*, p. 33. J. C. Chatterji, *La philosophie esotérique de l'Inde, ed. cit.*, p. 62: Each idea "is a tangible thing". Annie Besant, *The ancient wisdom, ed. cit.*, p. 63: "The vague loose thoughts which are so largely produced by undeveloped minds gather around themselves loose clouds of elemental essence . . . clinging round the astral bodies of persons whose magnetism attracts them—either good or evil—and after a while disintegrating . . ."

30 The Theosophists defend themselves against Materialism as well as against Idealism. They admit what is called today "the theory of identity", a theory according to which "Spirit and Matter are two aspects of one and the same Existence".

Chapter II

DREAMS

1. We do not ask the partisans of re-incarnation to answer all the questions raised by the physical experiences mentioned. Evidently "physical" experience will never be able to supply the clue to the mysteries of the "mental" or the "astral" world, since their nature, ex hypothesi, is different from that of the "physical" world. We only ask to be shown, by our actual experience, one single fact that could not be explained without the intervention of the "astral"or the "mental" world. For it is quite evident that if we are able to explain all the facts of our actual experience, without resorting to the mysterious world expounded by theosophy, the simple "principle of economy" forbids us to appeal to superfluous hypotheses. Now, is there in our actual experience any fact the explanation of which requires the intervention of the above mentioned worlds? Our opponents reply: Yes. It is the dream. Does it not withstand all efforts attempted by Science to reduce it to the laws of the physical world? What a richness of action and life under the seeming immobility of the sleeper! With terrific speed, he runs over enormous distances; with matchless agility he climbs the steepest mountains, or swings in the air. How can we justify such an anomaly? Must we not suppose that in this physical body which is motionless and dumb there is another body of a more subtle essence, which permeates it and performs the incredible feats of which it is dreaming?

On the other hand, do we not acquire during our sleep ideas which we totally lack when awake? For instance, we foresee the sickness which will come upon us much later; we receive warnings which will be most useful in the future. These facts, says Mrs. Besant, prove the existence of a second

[30]

conscious state which connects man with another world in-
terpenetrating the physical world, and consisting of more
subtle matter, which we call "astral"[1]. The matchless rapidity
with which psychic operations unfold during our sleep, declares the Head of the Theosophical Society, also proves that
while sleeping we are on a plane of life different from the
one which corresponds to the waking state. While asleep, the
astral body leaves the physical body and serves as a conscious organ in the higher world[2]. If we sometimes become
listless to the entreaties of the outside world, it is because
the astral body has then left the physical body[3]. Mrs. Besant
triumphantly concludes in this way: The state of waking
and the state of sleeping ought to be enough to convince
all men, from the learned philosopher to the ignorant savage,
of the difference between the two entities: the physical body
and the astral body.

2. To elaborate a complete theory of sleep would take
us too far from our subject. A few remarks will be enough.
Scientific research regarding sleep has proved that for the
most part the kind of animated pictures which form the web
of our dreams only reproduce, in a passive manner, the
phenomena observed in our active waking life. Bergson remarks that "a dream generally creates nothing"[4], "it is hardly
more than a resurrection of the past"[5].

However, all else that we see in our dream give us an impression of new and original creations. Why? For two reasons: 1) during sleep the sleeper is not completely deprived
of perception and impression; 2) his perceptions of a special
kind, on the one hand, and the memories and images that
his soul keeps, on the other, are incessantly changed under the
influence of different factors.

I would like to illustrate this thought by a personal experience. During the night of December 23, 1935, in Fras-
cati, where I then lived, I heard in my dream, some rather
mournful music which at once made me think of a funeral
ceremony. However, I could not see the people who were

singing. And the sinister melody continued with such persistence that I was soon bored with it. What monotony! It was always the repetition of the same tune! A feeling of uneasiness made me wake up. But, through the semi-consciousness of the first seconds of awakening, the everlasting melody continued. Then I realized that the serenader was a dog howling under the window.

Similar observations have been made by many scientists (J. Miller, A. Maury, H. Bergson, Corning Weygandt, G. F. Ladd, and others). A slight noise near the sleeper's ear is enough to make him hear in his dream the formidable noise of thunder. Some red and moving dots visible when awake through the closed eyelids often call forth in the mind of the sleeper fantastic scenes, full of color and movement. A candle lit in front of his closed eyes gives him the illusion of a conflagration. The simple feeling of his night garments at the very minute when he dreams of taking a walk, may produce the disagreeable impression that he went out indecently dressed. Should the sole of his foot lose contact with the sheet, owing to an unconscious movement, and his arm pressed against the bed begin to feel tired, the sleeper may easily imagine that he is floating upward in the air. Simple difficulties of digestion or circulation easily suggest to him the idea that someone is piercing him with a dagger.

In order to understand the transformations to which the sleeper's sensations are submitted, it is enough to remark that his psychic faculties are at work under extremely unfavorable conditions. His senses, for instance, are not in a condition to receive any impressions normally; through the narrow opening of the eyelids, encumbered with thick eyelashes, he is unable to perceive clearly the flame of a candle; he perceives only a vague light which resembles the red brilliancy of a fire. His ears stopped up, the one with the sheet, the other with the pillow, are in no position to recognize the peculiarities of a dog's howling. If he has no animals in

his home, is it not natural that he does not, in his sleep, think
of the cry of an animal, but rather of what he usually hears,
that of human voices? Finally the field of consciousness of
the sleeper is greatly reduced for lack of "antagonistic" perceptions, and it will be impossible for him to mentally em-
brace the whole complex of natural conditions which accompanies the cause of the excitation. Is it then surprising
that he should mistake the "image" for the "perception"?

Working on such fragmentary and chaotic matter, the intelligence cannot avoid mistakes and this is the reason for
erroneous judgments. On the other hand, there is no "de-
liberation" in sleep; the will loses its command of the other
faculties. Imagination being predominant under these circumstances builds its constructions at will, following its own
laws of association. In regard to the connection of facts, it
is chance that plays a most important part; scenes consisting
of simple images are characterized by a great instability;
they lack harmony and often look quite chaotic; things
without any interest emerge into full relief while other elements, which are of great value, are relegated to the background; the synthesis of ideas always lacks cohesion, through
default of logical connections. Consequently, there are many
contradictions. Desires which in the waking state were dormant in the soul and could not command attention because
of the "moral censure" of the will, now recover independence
and, to a certain extent, command the movements of the
imagination[6].

This emancipation of imagination and deep desires sometimes has happy results: some facts which had been completely wiped out from the memory, suddenly arise in the
mind. Images, ideas, suddenly group themselves together and
turn the thought toward paradoxical elaborations which may
sometimes even be taken for an inspiration of genius (for
genius is always paradoxical).

However, nothing compels us to admit in this case that a
superior force intervenes in our normal psychic life (or, ac-

cording to the expression of the re-incarnationists, in our "physical" life), and that this supposed intervention proves the existence of the "astral body" or the "astral consciousness". In fact, all the elements which constitute our dreams are taken from "physical" life, as is evident from the researches made by numerous psychologists (Calkin, Freud, Bernheim, Bergson, etc.). As to their association or synthesis, they show nothing that could not be submitted to the laws of psychology and logic as we know them in the waking state of our "physical" life.

3. Even those famous "prophecies" which our dreams supposedly bring us, are not an exception to this experience. For when they concern an illness which will assail us, they are a kind of obscure perception of the first symptoms of the forthcoming disease; and when they concern other events, they are nothing but an echo of certain ideas already more or less conceived in the waking state. But usually the "prophecies" which appear in dreams owe their credit only to an innate taste of the subject for fiction and to his lack of critical sense. For instance, if someone dreams that it is going to rain the next day, the chances are already great that this forecast will come true; they are about one to two in temperate climates; it will or it will not rain! One may say the same thing about all predictions for which the number of possible eventualities is very limited; for instance, success or failure, sickness or recovery, life or death, etc. What wonder then, if under these circumstances, a great number among that kind of predictions (about half) come true[7]? The other half remains unverified. But a person whose critical sense is not developed does not even notice that. He is so impressed by what he sees come true, that he loses sight of all false predictions; and he will go on sincerely repeating that all the events he sees in his dreams always materialize.

One fact will illustrate the illusion of which these people are the victims better than all theoretical reasoning. A friend told me, some time ago, that he always knew perfectly each morning, whether he would or would not receive a letter in the course of the day; that he knows it from his dreams of the previous night: if he sees a train in his dream, it is an infallible sign that he will receive a letter the next day; if not, he will not receive one. He was so convinced of the fact, that any discussion was useless. I used another method to show him his error. I asked him to write down every morning whether or not he had seen a train during the night and to write opposite it every evening whether or not he had received the expected letter. He promised to do so faithfully. Weeks went by without any news of the resulting verification. Finally, I went to the dreamer. "How are the dreams?" I asked. "It is very funny," he replied quite confused, "since we made that agreement, my dreams never come true anymore!"

If sober-minded people like my friend are so susceptible of being influenced by their dreams, what is to be expected from nervous, excited and unbalanced ones, the number of whom is ever increasing in our restless modern organization, over-crowded with machines? And what will the pathological subjects think, who are the prey of morbid illusions, of all kinds of amnesia, of hallucinations, and who yet seem to remain "capable" of the duties of practical life? Such psychic anomalies become more and more numerous[8].

As soon as we examine dreams with some critical sense, the so-called "prophecies" most frequently disappear in smoke. And what remains of them can be explained either by normal or abnormal psychology, or by "metapsychique"[9]. The theosophical theory is by no means necessary for this.

But this conclusion is very important here. Indeed, as we know, the theory of multiplicity of bodies (physical body, astral body, etc.) aims precisely at explaining why we do not remember what we accomplished before we came in to this world. And the objection of re-incarnation, based on "oblivion" of our former lives, thus gains all the more strength.

[1] *The ancient wisdom*, Adyar, 1939, pp. 60-82.

[2] *The ancient wisdom*, Adyar, 1939, pp. 60-82.

See Annie Besant, *When a man dies, shall he live again*, *A Lecture*, London, 1904, pp. 4-5.

[3] *The ancient wisdom*, Adyar, 1939, pp. 76-78.

[4] *L'énergie spirituelle, Le Rêve*, Paris, 1929, p. 99.

[5] *Bergson, l. c.*, p. 100.

[6] The theory that only the ideas stifled when one is awake by the censure of the will, become alive, has never been corroborated by experience.

[7] Numerous cases called phenomena of "telepathy", (when, for example, the wife "sees" her husband's death; the mother, her child's) belong to this class. One knows how often and how deeply women fear the death of their own loved ones.

[8] We do not want to mention the statements of dubious faith and accuracy, of dreams which never occurred. Such cases are unfortunately quite common, especially among hysterical people.

[9] In certain—quite exceptional—cases it could be explained by a supernatural intervention. See our study: *Metody badan zjawisk nadprzyodzonych* (Methods of studying supernatural facts, Krakow, 1933, fassim).

HYPNOSIS

1. In order to support their theory, shaken by conclusions of studies on "natural sleep" such as the one presented here, the advocates of re-incarnation appeal to the peculiarities of the "artificial sleep" commonly called "hypnosis". It is an unquestionable fact, they say, that during this sleep of a special nature, the subject may have precise memories of his past existence[1]. A certain woman, hypnotized by Colonel de Rochas, described to him in detail what she had done in the course of four different lives. Thus, by means of hypnosis, one should be able to restore to everyone the memory of his anterior existences.

2. This promise of the partisans of re-incarnation to bring back to us the memories of our past lives, thanks to hypnosis, could take its place among the "prophecies" mentioned before. For on what is it based? On the supposition that any person can be hypnotized. But, up to this day, no one has been able to justify this idea. And even though we could succeed in hypnotizing everybody, how would this support the thesis of the re-incarnationists? It is a fact that many hypnotized persons are opposed to this thesis. To mention only a few of them—and by no means among the less important ones!—the mediums who serve in the Anglo-Saxon spiritualistic meetings—reject positively the idea of re-incarnation: they never discover in themselves any memory of their past lives.

Other hypnotic subjects (the mediums of Allan Kardec's school) claim, it is true, to have such memories. But of what value are their testimonies? At the time of Mrs. Blavatsky and Mrs. Besant, hypnotism was still at its outset. One expected great things from this practice, which did not materialize. The recent experiments in hypnotism have taught us to handle this question with the greatest caution. This is not surprising if one is willing to examine the circumstances in which the subject is placed.

To be sure, he becomes much more sensitive than other people to certain stimuli; he often responds with a surprising facility to stimuli which do not even reach the threshold of normal consciousness and do not allow of any perception in normal subjects. He recovers memories which had seemed lost forever. But in connection with this, one should not lose sight of a most important fact: the will of the hypnotized person is never quite independent of the will of the hypnotizer; it is, so to speak, grafted on the latter's will in order to borrow from him, in a parasitical way, the strength to act, the courage necessary for decisions; in a word all that momentarily he is lacking[2]. Thus the hypnotizer becomes to him (especially if such practices between them are repeated) a real spiritual father whom he finally cannot dispense with, and who becomes an acting element of his own personality.

Is it surprising, under these conditions, that the subject guesses all the wishes and all the intentions of this powerful director, that he accepts all his ideas and principles? If the hypnotizer is an advocate of re-incarnation, or suggests by his questions the least desire to discover in the "hypnotized subject" memories of former lives, the subject will not fail to give him satisfactory answers.

Such "suggestions" are especially to be feared, when it is a case of subjects who, in waking state, already believe in re-incarnation. And this consideration makes possible the explanation of a fact that, at first sight, is quite disconcerting: the spirits which manifest themselves at the meetings of the Spiritualists of Allan Kardec's School ("latin spiritualism") assert with strong conviction the truth of re-incarnation; but those who appear at the meetings of the Anglo-Saxon spiritualists deny it with no less conviction. This kind of schism (which, of course, highly embarrasses the Spiritualists) is easily accounted for by the simple fact that the dead do not really attend the meetings of the spiritualists, only the "media". They quite evidently speak according to their own ideas and according to the suggestions received from their circle. The Anglo-Saxon denies re-incarnation, simply because Anglo-Saxon Spiritualism rejects it, while the Latin medium supports re-incarnation because Latin Spiritualism asserts it. Whoever knows hypnosis, not from legends, nor from reading books, but practically, from direct observation, will discount the evidences in favor of re-incarnation which Colonel de Rochas drew from his practice. The most enlightened partisans of re-incarnation admit this nowadays. "In 1911", one of them says, "Colonel de Rochas published a book in which he mentions a few facts of reminiscence provoked by means of suggestion ... however, these facts are not convincing, for suggestion may have produced illusions corresponding to what he was expecting"[3].

From the fact that a subject hypnotized by a re-incarnationist tells details of a former life as if it were present to him, and even assumes attitudes corresponding to the situation, we should not conclude that his real memory is undertaking such a distant exploration and is really posting itself on the life of other worlds, as some adepts of this doctrine claim. If the hypnotized subject spontaneously assumes attitudes corresponding to any social situation he may have enjoyed in a former re-incarnation, this is fully explained by the law, very well known in psychology, called by the very vague name, the "law of motricity of ideas". Our ideas are not inert. They ought, on the contrary, to be considered as dynamic points, as centres of action; they are acts or energies of the spirit; this is why they necessarily stir up in us deep and immanent tendencies which extend themselves and naturally develop into external actions and movements. If I think of a dog, said a patient to Peter Janet, I feel the urge to fall upon a man and bite him[4]. If I think of a cigarette, said another, I stretch out my hands, in spite of myself, towards the tobacco[5].

Thus, if by means of hypnosis, we succeed in suggesting to someone that he is a soldier, he will naturally take a soldier's attitude. If we suggest to him that he is a king, he will change his posture in order to conform himself to his new dignity and will behave as he imagines a king should do. Let us now convince him, while he is still in the hypnotic state, that he is living through one of his former incarnations: he will at once assume the attitude corresponding to any suggested situation, which he thinks required by this new suggestion.

From a psychological point of view, hypnosis is a state of deep distraction caused by the shrinking of the conscious background; it is a kind of "monoideism". Consequently, it is not surprising, after the idea has been imposed on a subject in whose consciousness it does not find any "antagonistic" image, that this idea unfolds freely and completely, that is to say, into action, into movement. If the hands of a hypnotized person are crossed as if he were about to receive Holy Communion, he will kneel down and automatically go through the whole series of gestures generally accompanying this religious act. If convinced that he is a child, he will imitate the tone of a child, his way of speaking, his caprices; will try to walk on all fours, etc.

Mr. de Rochas' experiments with hypnotic subjects, which the re-incarnationists like to recall, are devoid of any value[6].

1 Annie Besant, *The ancient wisdom*, Adyar, 1939, pp. 220-221.
2 We do not mean that the hypnotizer can do whatever he likes with his subject, who sometimes resists him to an hysterical crisis.
3 W. Lutoslawski, *Preesistenza e Rincarnazione ed. cit.*, p. 47.
4 *Les obsessions et la psychasthénie*, Paris, 1919, p. 82.
5 *Ibid.* This phenomenon is especially manifest in "emotional", "impulsive", "absent-minded" people.
6 The "law of motricity of ideas" explains (to some extent) many "marvels": Cumberlandism, the divinatory rod, turning tables, nostalgies, etc.
   Some of these facts have already been discussed in another work (*Konnersreuth w swietle nauki i religji*, Krakow, 1913, pp. 243-248). One more word about the divinatory rod. People go into raptures at the sight of its marvelous power. It permits us, so they claim, to discover springs, mineral beds; to

foresee the sex of a child to come; to diagnose diseases, etc. It is becoming more and more popular. But it is only the tool of a prejudice. When someone is looking for water in a field; when he wants a spring to gush out, he calls the "water diviner". The diviner takes a rod, either forked or not, but very sensitive to exterior excitations, to motions. He carries it to the field, which he first looks over. He has already scanned many in the same way. This is his profession (and not everybody can practice it). He makes mistakes, and his admirers admit it. Many a time he has had the soil upturned and nothing came of it but earth. But he acquired a certain experience in subterraneous waters. He looks carefully, and suddenly he thinks: "In this soil, one might discover water." This thought is accompanied by a shiver of the body (a consequence of the law of motricity of ideas), an imperceptible quiver, of which he is not conscious, but which also agitates the rod, the magic rod, sensitive to the least motion. He looks at it and is surprised to see it move. "The water cannot be far away," he thinks. This very thought increases the trembling of his hands. "Decidedly, I am getting nearer and nearer." Finally, he stops: "Open the earth here!" he orders. Often water is found; often not. But we do not like this second evidence, we ignore it. The water diviner may be mistaken—errare humanum est. . . .

CHAPTER IV

REMINISCENCES OF CHILDREN

1. The advocates of re-incarnation do not admit defeat on this subject of reminiscences. Look at children, they say. Their brains are, so to speak, more plastic than ours; this is why they retain the memories of their past lives more faithfully. Ask them what they used to do formerly, fifty years ago, for instance, or a hundred years ago. You will hear stories full of dramatic animation. These are not "invented", as is commonly believed. They are "reminiscences" of previous incarnations[1]. There is hardly any essay on re-incarnation which does not put forward this argument. Consequently we must give special attention to the child's "reminiscences."

2. The first difficulty is as follows: why should not all children have reminiscences? The answer is: because the child's memory is not always perfect; according to the time which has elapsed between a person's death and his re-incarnation, his memory will, more or less faithfully, retain the facts of his past life. Now there are souls which are only re-incarnated after centuries, or even thousands of years. During a long former life they had collected so many valuable experiences that, after death, they needed a long period of "rest" in order to "assimilate these experiences," to convert them into "faculties, powers, tendencies". Other souls have scarcely profited by the lessons of their former life. Before reaching maturity they were snatched from the body, due to some untimely accident; the experience they may have accumulated in that life is negligible; a short "rest" among the "blessed spirits" will be enough to transmute these few lessons into a slight spiritual betterment. Among the souls of this kind we find, for instance, those of young soldiers killed in war. "We may hope," says Irv. S. Cooper, "that the chil-

dren born between 1914 and 1920 will keep most vivid memories of the First World War; if our conjecture proves to be true, re-incarnation will be demonstrated with such evidence that it will be impossible for any one to doubt it"[2].

Decidedly, advocates of re-incarnation are not very hard to please. It is easy enough to foresee that the children born during a war, or immediately after, will often speak of it because they will have heard terrible stories about it from their earliest childhood and they may have seen the funerals of some who died during it. The sensitive soul of the child will have lived in the atmosphere of that great catastrophe and derived from it plentiful matter for day-dreaming.

Dreams with something like a suggestion of previous existences occur almost necessarily in the lives of children. Sometimes it may be difficult even for an adult to believe that he has never lived in other worlds before reaching this one, and that after his death, he will not live again in other places. Where was he thousands of years before his birth? What was he doing then? Thousands of years will follow his death: where will he be? What will he do during this long future? In spite of himself a cry of protest and rebellion escapes his soul. And this inward storm dies down only when, thanks to an effort of will-power, he succeeds in silencing his sensibility; when he accepts—if not whole-heartedly at least from necessity—the destiny of Nature, the will of God.

But a child cannot possibly make this effort. Moreover his intelligence does not suggest to him any reason to do so. He lives in the present, and is not interested in the future or the past; when one draws his attention to them, he thinks of them in the light of the present hour into which both, so to speak, melt for him. For a child, reality hardly differs from fiction, and everything is a continuous game: the child plays with everything at all times. What exists at the present has always existed. He himself has always existed, and he could hardly believe that he will not always exist. Thus when he has to take up his secular existence, past or future, he will not experience any special difficulty because his critical sense is not yet awake. Fiction will fill every gap created by lack of judgment.

One often speaks of the natural truthfulness of the child, but this so-called love of truth is grossly exaggerated. Suppose we listen to a child telling the story of events we have witnessed. How easily he embellishes it while distorting the facts! Without any intention of deceiving us, without imagining clever lies (which would require an intellectual effort he cannot make as yet), the child gives himself over to numerous petty lies for no other reason than the very weakness of his judgment, the lack of critical spirit mentioned before.

Let us add that the child is too weak to organize a defense against the invasion of other people's ideas; he accepts them; he is readily open to suggestions, and this is often due to the way he is asked questions. This is why it has been observed that in those countries where re-incarnation is generally admitted (in India, for instance), children's reminiscences of former incarnations are especially frequent.

3. Let us continue our investigation. At the approximate age of seven, the child loses "the memory of his past lives". Why? According to the believers in re-incarnation this is the result of the "censure" exercised by adults who make the mistake of blaming and punishing him for all these "lies" which he imagines. Is this explanation satisfactory to us? Do we not remember many actions of our youth for which we were "blamed" and "punished"? But re-incarnation itself, whoever remembers it?

Other re-incarnationists give different explanations. Around his seventh year, they say, the brain of a child loses its "freshness" and its "plasticity" under the influence of outside impressions, and the necessities of practical life begin to absorb his attention. This explanation has no value. When attention is focused on a few impressions, or on some action, memory, it is true, becomes less apt to "register" new facts, or to "recall" old perceptions. But, in the case we are interested in, there is no question of "registering" new facts nor of "recalling" old ones, but of the complete non-existence of these old facts. This is what remains to be explained. Where would this kind of negative "selectivity" come from, which memory would manifest regarding memories exclusively pertaining to re-incarnation? After all, we remember a number of things which we thought about before the age of seven!

If the child loses the "memories" pertaining to re-incarnation at about the age of seven, this is due to the fact that, approximately at this age, the critical sense awakes in him; he begins to distinguish between truth and falsehood; to recognize more clearly the limits between the real and the fictional world; to emerge from the "egocentrism" in which psychic faculties in an embryonic state have held him a prisoner. Condemned at first to use almost exclusively his own senses, he began to judge everything in the light of his personal pleasure; people, and objects as well, at first did not mean anything to him except as tools of his pleasure and caprices. If one tried to correct him, he would fill the house with such cries, that everyone hurried to satisfy the wishes of the little autocrat. He was fully conscious of his power and used it. He sometimes became a real tyrant, and was cruel to his cat, his dog or some bird that had fallen in the garden.

The advocates of re-incarnation emphasize the state of barbarism in childhood. According to them, it is a manifestation of a "reminiscence" of the "state of barbarism" experienced by him. Such an affirmation is decidedly too hasty. The child's cruelty is easily explained by his inability to appreciate in full other people's situations; in general, he does not even suspect that his way of handling animals, his favorite recreation, might be disagreeable to them. In fact, in order to realize other people's sufferings one must not only have gone through suffering oneself, an experience which the child has not had, but also be able to imagine oneself in other people's circumstances, and consequently, know how to effect abstraction. Now, the child is unable to do so, for he can use only his senses, his essentially "intuitive" faculties.

The comparison between the child and the barbarian is based on ideas which have long been considered obsolete, namely: that the child, from a psychological point of view, is a small adult. But, in truth, the child is an individual "sui generis": his way of observing the world, his method of evaluating everything, have nothing in common with the behavior of the adult. Even his religion has a special character; it is a "childish religion": he believes firmly that Christmas presents are brought by the Child Jesus; this truth is as much a part of his creed as all the religious truths of the Holy Scriptures. He does not discriminate at all between them.

Such is the true character of childhood. And all we have said shows clearly how weak is the argument in favor of re-incarnation borrowed from the "character of children". Any evidence is worthy of belief only in proportion as the witness is able to tell the truth. The child is unable to do so. That is the whole point.

1 See Annie Besant, *The ancient wisdom*, Adyar, 1939, p. 222.
2 *Reincarnation the hope of the world*, Krotona, 1920, p. 86.

CHAPTER V

MEMORIES OF THE "INITIATED"

1. Neither a sleeping man, nor a man in hypnosis, nor a child, can win our confidence when it is a question of proving the truth of re-incarnation, for all three of them are precisely in those conditions which make one suspect any evidence they can give; all three are dreaming although each one dreams in his own way. Some advocates of re-incarnation more or less suspect this fact. That is why they try hard to demonstrate that some people have memories of their past lives when they are in full command of their faculties. In this connection they name Pythagoras and Empedocles, Buddha, Mrs. Blavatsky, the founder of the Theosophic Society, Annie Besant, and a few other famous re-incarnationists.

2. To begin with Pythagoras, let us first notice that his memories of past lives are not such a certain fact as some people are wont to believe. Let us listen to Diogenes of Laerte: "Heraclitia of the Pontus reminds us that Pythagoras used to say he was formerly Ethalides; . . . that Mercury encouraged him to ask for whatever he wished. . . . So he asked to be able to remember all that might happen to him— whether dead or alive. . . . One day, he was incarnated in the body of Euphorbus and wounded by Menalaus. While he was Euphorbus, he said he had formerly been Ethalides and had obtained from Mercury the favor that his soul might pass through eternal transmigrations and into whatever plants or animals it pleased. . . . After Euphorbus' death, his soul lived in the body of Hermotimus . . . . and then in that of Pyrrhus, a fisherman of Delos"[1].

This whole story looks just like one of those legends which are so easily attached to the names of famous men. In any case, it contains a number of mythological elements. In the same story, e.g., it is said that Pythagoras had "a golden leg"[2], that he was considered as a God[3] and so on. The life of Pythagoras written by Porphyry and Iamblichus does not merit greater faith than that by Diogenes Laertius. Modern scholars generally admit that the sources which they used are not very reliable. Indeed, Porphyry used Nicomachus and Antonius Diogenes, the latter the author of the Marvels from beyond Thule parodied by Lucian in his Vera Historia. Iamblichus used a work by Nicomachus of Gerasa, an arithmetician, and the romance of Appolonius of Thyana.

Even supposing that it originated, in its main lines, in authentic statements by Pythagoras, the question remains: in what measure does a story of this kind deserve to command attention? A remark on this point by Diogenes Laertius is very significant. "Aristoxenus says that Pythagoras took most of his moral doctrines from Themistoclea, the priestess at Delphi"[4]. Unfortunately, we know neither Themistoclea nor the nature of the influence she may have had on him. Pythagoras, in order to corroborate such an assertion, has given no other evidence than the "ipse dixit", says Mr. F. Myers'[5].

The reincarnationists object. Did Pythagoras really not leave us any criterion which would allow us to verify his identity with Euphorbus? He recognized in Apollo's temple the shield that he had carried in former times and which had belonged to Euphorbus[6]! Here is Tertullian's answer to this: If Pythagoras really recognized this shield, thanks to some secret characteristics, it follows at most that he knew this object but not that he had this knowledge from an anterior existence; in fact, he may secretly have learned from some one all the particularities of this shield; he even may have bribed the Keeper so as to study the question at will[7]. Eneas Gazaeus calls Pythagoras' story an "arrogant fable"[8] invented to "prove what he asserted"[9]. Lactantius is almost of the same opinion[10]. Saint Augustine admits that Pythagoras may have been the victim of an illusion: "In sleep," he says, "it also seems to us that we have seen or done a certain thing, that we have neither seen nor done."[11]

It must be agreed that those authors who accuse Pythagoras of having told a lie are unable to prove it. On the other hand, Pythagoras has in no way demonstrated what he asserted. St. Augustine's suggestion seems to us to be the most plausible. Illusions of memory are quite frequent and well known to psychologists; we shall quote some later. Let us add one last remark, which is decisive for our question. The soul of Pythagoras is said to have been incarnated not only in men, but also in "whatever plants and animals it pleased"[12]. Now the modern believers in re-incarnation teach that the human soul cannot be re-incarnated in animals or plants[13].

3. Let us pass on to another philosopher, Empedocles. We know too little about his life to be able to weigh the probabilities of exactitude in his so-called "memories" concerning former existences. Whatever we know about him is rather of a nature to make us sceptical. In fact, Empedocles, at least as described by Diogenes Laertius, is a very strange character. He is said to have been extremely vain; he even dared to take the title of God and demanded sacrifices[14]. In order to attract public attention and make people believe that he really had become a god, so Hippobotus tells us, the idea came to him one day to throw himself "into the Etna crater"[15]. Let us not forget that in Aristotle's works, Empedocles is already considered an "epileptic"[16].

4. Buddha is also said to have spoken of his re-incarnation. The value of his testimony is evident from what we have said before on this matter[17]. One would have to be very easily influenced in order to accept the proof that Mrs. Blavatsky offers in support of Buddha's re-incarnation in her book *Isis unveiled*: "a child cried out that he was Buddha's re-incarnation"[18]. After what has been said before about the "child's mentality", any commentary on this argument is superfluous.

Apollonius of Tyana, a famous "thaumaturge and Pythagorian prophet"[19], Ovid, the great Latin poet, and the emperor Julian the Apostate[20], are also said to have had memories of previous lives; Ovid is said to have taken part in the Trojan War; Julian the Apostate thought that he had been Alexander the Great in another era. But the only evidence they have left us of their claims is the famous ipse dixit.

5. According to the Theosophists, the founder of their Society, Mrs. Blavatsky was also conscious of her past life. This fact calls for all the more attention as it is a question of a person of our own time, whom we know, not through the medium of mythology and legends, but through recent and precise testimonies. Although she liked to wrap herself in mystery and surround herself with fiction, we have sufficient knowledge of her life.

Mrs. Blavatsky had an "unbearable" disposition from her early infancy[21]; "for a mere trifle she would go into a violent fit of anger"[22], "she was at war with her whole family"[23]. Later, she indulged excessively in the practices of spiritism; she took part in revolutionary movements and joined the freemasonry. Then she gave herself up to the good care of a certain Michal, who developed in her the faculties of a medium[24]. This adventurous life resulted in a "splitting of her personality", a phenomenon to which Michal himself never referred without a certain dread[25]. When she appeared on the stage (in Cairo and in America) to offer demonstrations, she committed such frauds that she was exposed and had to shamefully give up this method of propaganda. But she never could resist her love of fiction. Guenon reveals that she spoke a great deal of a certain trip to Tibet, a country upon which she had never set eyes[26].

These are all symptoms of chronic psychopathy. "Exceptional mediumnic" faculties are found especially in people affected with psychic neuroses, so much so that in proportion as they are cured they lose pari passu these faculties. The same is true of "the splitting of the personality", as well as an exaggerated egotism that makes the person "unbearable" to her entourage, and causes her to wrap herself in constant fictions and lies, which constitute the characteristic symptoms of a psychopathic state.

Now, since we are compelled to admit Mrs. Blavatsky's unbalanced mentality, it is impossible for us to give any credence to her testimony when she speaks of her preceding re-incarnations. Who knows whether she does not intend to mystify us as she systematically did so many others? Or she might try to deceive us unconsciously. One knows that, from her adolescence on, she always felt the presence of a mysterious being who accompanied her everywhere. Such a revelation should put us on our guard. Mrs. Blavatsky was subject to hallucinations. Does not her impression of having lived several times previously in this world belong to the same class of hallucinations?

6. Let us now pass on to Mrs. Annie Besant, who was the president of the Theosophical Society for many years. Even as a child, Mrs. Besant was a victim of hallucinations for which her family blamed her quite severely. They only considered them as a troublesome tendency to "lying"[27]; her temperament was characterized by a propensity for "dreaming"[28], by an acute susceptibility and excessive ambition. Selfishness, which is natural to everyone, assumed with her absolutely abnormal forms; she was tormented by a kind of megalomania, which inspired her with the desire to found "a religion of the future" and estranged her more and more from social life. She was "impulsive, very hot-tempered, and proud as Lucifer"[29] (these are her own words). Moreover, she was haunted by sudden terror of some "vague, misty" beings whose presence she felt around her, and she was seized by anguish at the mere thought she might see them[30].

These few facts are so many impartial witnesses, since they are all taken from an autobiography. They entitle the psychiatrist to diagnose in Mrs. Besant a somewhat unbalanced mentality. One question only remains for discussion: into what category of patients should Mrs. Besant be placed? But this question does not seem to us to be very important, all the more so as the actual classifications of psychic disorders are under reconsideration. The main thing is that Mrs. Besant was not normal from a psychic point of view. And this is enough to warn us only to accept the tales of her memories of a former existence with extreme caution.

7. According to the advocates of re-incarnation, Goethe also was conscious of having lived several times. But this is only because he wrote: "Surely, I must have lived already before the Emperor Hadrian, for everything Roman attracts me with inexpressible force"[31].

Do not the reincarnationists really draw from these words a much too hasty conclusion? Are they quite sure of what Goethe meant? His certitude of having really lived in Rome, or only a great liking for everything Roman? The reply to the first question remains very doubtful.

But we still have another observation to make on this "testimony" of Goethe's, even supposing that the famous poet ever had the idea that the re-incarnationists attribute to him.

Although the rather general opinion which considers genius as a "sublime madness" does not deserve any more credit than most of such brilliant formulas, one may, however, wonder whether some particular psychic anomalies do not transform a simple talent into that exceptional thing which is called genius. Some psychic anomalies, to be sure, concentrate the entire mental activity on one aspiration alone, which thus is hypertrophied, setting to work all the forces of the soul and driving them, so to speak, to carry by storm that conquest which is the realization of a great dream. One does not have to be a disciple of Lombroso to admit that many genii have been affected with serious psychic disorders[32]. Goethe certainly is one of them. Here is his psychological physiognomy as described by J. Grasset[33]: Goethe wrote many of his poems in a state which resembled somnambulism; he suddenly passed from excessive joy to the deepest melancholy; no doubt a grave hereditary blemish must have lain upon him; his sister was a little more than peculiar; his grandfather had hallucinations; he himself was subject to hypochondria, to delirium, and to fits of anger which nothing justified; he often suffered from a kind of spleen and was assailed by ideas of suicide. He states that he once saw his own image coming to meet him. Mobius compared his periods of production to the phases of the disease known as circular madness. In Goethe's works many degenerates, hysterical, and even mad people appear. Now he did not study these pathological cases in lunatic asylums, which filled him with great awe; he observed them in himself and in his most intimate circle. This should put us on our guard. One should not accept too simply Goethe's testimony as to his "reminiscences". He may have been the victim of illusions.

8. Some believers in re-incarnation also mention the case of Alexander Dumas, Junior, who had memories of past lives. Really, the re-incarnationists have little good fortune. In 1859, Dumas, Junior, had an illness that the doctors declared to be "ultra-nervous", which is very significant. Here is what his father had to say in this connection: "Alexander is very sick . . . for two days he has been kneeling in the middle of his room without our being able to make him get up. . . . Two days before this, hearing his father snoring in an adjoining room produced such a state of nervous excitement, that he thought of killing his father and could not have resisted this idea if he had not knelt down. . . ." Dumas remained in this state of insanity for a year. After recovering from this cerebral illness, Dumas went through a violent crisis of mysticism. Finally, he conquered the trouble. However, in 1873, after writing La Femme de Claude, he had another short attack[34]. The testimony of Alexander Dumas, Junior, then can only be accepted with the greatest discretion.

9. Among those who are supposed to have enjoyed the signal privilege of remembering their former lives, is Swedenborg. But we do not intend to discuss his case at length.

Swedenborg, as Gilbert Baillet plainly proves in an extensive study of his case, was, from the psychic point of view, seriously ill; he was suffering from persistent hallucinations[35]. Were not his so-called memories of former existences a part of these? It is impossible to prove the contrary.

10. We consider it absolutely futile to discuss in detail all the facts mentioned by the re-incarnationists in their efforts to prove the value of these alleged "memories" of past existences. To examine scrupulously only a few of these examples is enough to form an opinion about all of them—and let us hasten to add—not in the name of the principle ex uno disce omnes, for everyone knows that this principle is logically wrong and morally unjust; but, on the contrary, out of regard for the scientific method—which the re-incarnationists throw to the winds with the greatest unconcern, as soon as they mention any one of these examples.

Here is one case: A lady in Chicago drew designs of an incontestably Egyptian style. Now some Egyptologists determined the exact period of which these designs were allegedly only a "reminiscence".[36] Far be it from us to suspect the competency of the Egyptologists. We prefer to bow to to the authority of specialists. But in the name of psychology alone, we want to express our reservation. Before admitting the pertinency of alleged "memories of past incarnations" one should first prove that Mrs. Field (this was the name of that lady) had never seen any picture of the monuments of old Egypt; a very difficult task, for it is almost impossible that any well educated person should never have seen any illustrations of this kind. Moreover, it would be appropriate to study with care Mrs. Field's character, her psychic faculties, the degree of her usual love of truth, her taste for imaginative things, etc. It would still be necessary to prove that she did not draw her designs in a state of somnambulism (when old semi-conscious perceptions suddenly force themselves on consciousness in the form of strangely precise memories). One more observation: how could one demonstrate that such designs drawn by Mrs. Field really represented a particular house which she had seen in the course of a past life?

Another lady, named Laure Raynaud, is said to have remembered having lived a former life in a country bathed in sunshine; she saw her house and she remembered having died there "young"! We are also told that Mrs. Raynaud recognized in the neighborhood of Genoa the environment in which she had passed her former infancy. She talked to those who lived in a neighboring house and gave orders for researches which resulted in the following discovery: a young girl had died there October 21, 1809.

It is a great pity that we are not better acquainted with Mrs. Raynaud's psychology and morality. But did she not supply "objective criterions"? say the re-incarnationists. No doubt: but what are they worth? She remembered living in a country full of sunshine. How many of those are there in the world? But she knew that she had died "young". Really, what a pity she was not more exact! The adjective "young" has as elastic a meaning as the adjective "old", and that is saying a great deal; a man generally considers "old" anyone who is 10 years older than he is. Mrs. Raynaud lived there "in other days". About when? One might suppose a priori that in an old building which had welcomed under its roof several generations, one would surely find someone who had died there "young"! We are also told that Mrs. Raynaud recognized the house. How? By the help of what criteria? Was it by the "feeling" one has when one recovers contact with some thing formerly familiar? But the confusions of object which are sometimes due to this kind of sentiment, are explained by the psychology of "affective life", and especially by the laws of "sympathy": whatever we like very much becomes, so to speak, "ours"!; it stirs up in us an impression of familiarity which normally could only result from a long existence in common. And if the person who feels this impression does not possess a sufficiently strong will and a

[55]

critical mind, he might easily be mistaken and become the victim of an illusion.

One more "fact" which is invoked in order to prove the truth of re-incarnation. A Hindu girl (Ramkoli, the daughter of a Brahman) looked in a distant village (Maglabad), for the "sons" whom she had in a preceding re-incarnation. She found them!

Let us overlook the difficulty resulting from the fact that we know almost nothing about this young girl: neither her mental state, nor her temperament, nor her character. However, we know one thing which is very valuable when it is a question of judging her testimony: she was the daughter of a Brahman. She lived in the atmosphere of re-incarnation. Is it surprising that one day she conceived the idea of looking for "her children"? She finds them, she finds three! But by what means was she able to verify their identity? By means of their resemblance?

How many times do we happen to find a mineral seemingly alike in every way to another one which we have already seen before? We never even think of finding out the common origin of those two stones. Moreover, does it not often happen that two people who are living simultaneously have a striking resemblance?[37]

Finally, according to the re-incarnationists, the same individual may in the course of two successive re-incarnations possess entirely different personal characteristics: Euphorbus who took part in the Trojan War, was absolutely different from Pythagoras, the philosopher; neither one had anything in common with the fisherman, Pyrrhus, and yet, according to the re-incarnationists, we are dealing, under these three names, with one and the same individual.

11. We will sum up in a few words: the formal memory of past lives of which some people boast, offers no guarantee of certitude: the affections of memory, the phenomena of suggestion and auto-suggestion are quite sufficient to explain all such impressions. Moreover, if it is supposed that the

manifestations of that kind of "memory" are so few that they may rightly be considered as "exceptions corroborating the rule", one understands our scepticism regarding them.

12. The pathological character of all these "formal memories" seems to be corroborated by the manifestations of megalomania which generally accompany them. It is not without some shame that the wisest advocates of re-incarnation admit it. We find in certain circles, says the famous Occultist Papus (G. A. V. Encausse) worthy people who believe themselves to be Molière, Racine or Richelieu, not to mention Orpheus or Homer[38]. There are hardly any circles where Alexander the Great and Napoleon do not daily come back to dwell in the bodies of retired captains or colonels.

The wife of the famous heresiarch, Simon the Samaritan, had been Helen of Troy[39]. Daniel Douglas Home found at least twelve different women each of whom believed that she was a re-incarnation of Marie Antoinette; six or seven others claimed at the same time their identity with Mary Stuart; about twenty persons insisted at any cost, that they were Alexander the Great, but never a plain John Smith[40]. Anne Kingsford and Edoard Maitland, writes Fr. W. H. Myers, pretend to have been respectively the Holy Virgin and St. John[41].

In order to counteract this megalomania which threatens to disgrace the doctrine of re-incarnation for any person with a minimum of critical sense, some re-incarnationists (among whom Papus) emphasize that the memories of our former existences do not generally bring with them a knowledge of details, and that they remain vague and fragmentary. Thus, for instance, we may remember having lived at the time of Alexander, or Caesar, without, however, knowing all the particulars of that former existence. It may be that we were entrusted with most insignificant functions by those great men. After all, adds Papus somewhat sarcastically, it would be severe punishment for all these famous men, to have to come down into such unimportant characters as plain citizens, or captains and their wives[42].

Alas, this elementary remark of good sense did not prove very efficient in reality. The alleged "consciousness of former existences" most often comes from an abnormal psychic condition, which is unmoved by censure; all the more so as this alleged "consciousness" is considered by those who are affected by it as an immediate "intuition" of experience. Now, contra experimentum nullum argumentum! In other cases it results from long and patient efforts made to develop it. It originates in certain action exercised on the cerebellum and pineal glandule, in a long meditation[43], and assiduous prayer[44] most often—let us hasten to say—conceived in the theosophical manner, that is to say a "prayer of the will"[45], "a prayer which is rather a command of the soul" than a real prayer or a "petition"[46].

The "consciousness of experienced re-incarnations" is then the result of acquired habits, of the acquisition of a special "mentality" which is artificially created in the subject: in one word, it is the result of training. This is why it would be as difficult to change the conviction of any person of his former incarnations as to change his soul.

This last remark sufficiently explains why the true re-incarnationists are invincible. Shut in the fortress of their illusions, of their hallucinations, which, in their simplicity, they believe to be the results of an immediate "experience", of an "illumination", they defy all the assaults of reason.

The principle of "letting the living images unfold before the trained reason" which the re-incarnationists profess, is not too bad in itself. If someone does not clearly recall some detail of his life, he will do well to put himself in the situation of an "onlooker"—who passively observes the passing of all these images in his soul; every one of them, by reason of that "immanent dynamism" mentioned elsewhere, tends to revive, in its integrity, the perception of which it is, in a sense, only an extension and similar to "a secondary state";

there among the many details which thus come back to psychic life, one often finds the one looked for.

As a mnemonic process, let us repeat, this is not bad. However, it should be used with great caution. One must make sure, in particular, that some details, invented by the imagination do not insinuate themselves, through parasitic associations, into the flux of real images. One must at any cost check on the spectator's "observation" by the control of the "actor".

Now, in the case we are studying, it is the re-incarnationist himself who plays the part of surveyor. And he is a firm believer in re-incarnation. Therefore, he will interfere, often unconsciously, each time the images seem to depart from the desired reminiscences. The wish to find a confirmation of his belief by the method of "letting the living images unfold themselves. . . ." will bring into this mnemonic flux what we call "a psychic attitude"; will impose on the chaos of images a certain order, will give them direction. And the re-incarnationist will always find in the end what he was looking for: "memories" of former incarnations.

1 *De clarorum Philosophorum vitis, lib.* VIII, 4-5 (ed. Parisiis, 1850), pp. 205-206.

2 Diogenes Laertius, *ibid.*, lib., VIII, 11. See also *Iamblichi De Pythagorica Vita* XXVIII 135; XIX, 92. *Porphyri De Vita Pythagorae.* 28.

3 Diog. Laertius, *ibid.*, VIII, 11; Iamblichi, *ibid.*, XIX, 92.

4 Diogenes Laertius, *ibid.*, VIII, 8.

5 *Human Personality and Its Survival of Bodily Death*, II vol, NY 1903, pp. 11, 136.

6 Diogenes Laertius, *ibid.*, VIII, 5.

7 *De Anima*, C. 28; P. G. 697.

8 *Op. cit.*, P. G. 85, 902.

9 *Ibid.*

10 *Divinarum Institutionum* liber III: *De Falsa sapientia philosophorum*, cap. 18; P. L. 6, 409-410.

11 *De Genesi ad litteram* VII, 11; P.L.34, 361; *De Trinit.* XII, 15; P.L.42, 1912.

12 Diogenes Laertius, *ibid.*, lib. VIII, 4.

13 See some quotations in our *Introduction.*

14 Empedocles asserted that "the soul inhabits every kind of form of animals and plants. According, he thus expresses himself: "For once I was a boy and once a girl, A bush, a bird, a fish who swims the sea" (Diogenes Laertius, *ibid.*, lib. VIII, 77).

15 Diogenes Laertius, *ibid.*, VIII, 69-70.

16 Problems, Book XXX, 1, 953, a 10-29. J. Grasset, *Demi-fous et demi-responsables*, Paris, 1907, p. 183 See also Cicero, *Tusc. Disp.* I, 33, and Plutarch, *Vit. Lysandri*, 2.

17 See above, First Part, Chapter I.

18 Vol. I, Science, New York, 1893, p. 437.

19 Cf. Fr. Ueberweg, *Grundriss der Geschichte der Philosophie*, I, 1926, p. 513.

20 Cf. K. O. Schmidt, *Die Wiederverkörperung der Seele,* (without date), p. 43.

21 René Guenon, *Le Théosophisme*, Paris, II éd., p. 11.

22 *Ibid.*, p. 11.

23 *Ibid.*, p. 12.

24 *Ibid.*, p. 15.

25 *Ibid.*, p. 14.

26 Guenon, *op. cit.*, pp. 15, 26, 27, 30.

27 *An Autobiography*, London, 1920, p. 25, 40.

28 *Ibid.*, pp. 25, 40.

29 *Ibid.*, p. 81.

30 *Ibid.*, p. 45: "The things that really frightened me were vague, misty presences that I felt were near, but could not see. They were so real that I knew just where they were in the room, and the peculiar terror they excited lay largely in the feeling that I was just going to see them. If by chance I came across a ghost story, it haunted me for months, for I saw whatever unpleasant spectre was described; and there was one horrid old woman in a tale by Sir Walter Scott, who glided up to the foot of your bed and sprang on it in some eerie fashion and glared at you, and who made my going to bed a terror to me for many weeks. I can still recall the feeling so vividly that it almost frightens me now" (*ibid.*, p. 45). See also Annie Besant, *The ancient wisdom, ed. cit.*, p. 66-67.

31 K. O. Schmidt, *op. cit.*, p. 43.

32 In the work *Problemata* which is attributed to Aristotle, we read as follows: "Why is it that all those who have become eminent in philosophy, or politics, or poetry, or the arts, are clearly of an atrabilious temperament, and some of them to such an extent as to be affected by diseases caused by black bile" (XXX, 1, 953 a 10-13). "Among men of recent times Empedocles, Plato and Socrates, and many numerous other well-known men, and also most of the poets" are said to have suffered from epileptic afflictions, which were called by the ancients "the sacred disease" (Problemata, ibid., 953 a 26-29; 15-17).

33 *Demi-fous et Demi-responsables.* Paris, Alcan, 1914, (IIIe éd.), p. 177.

34 *Une maladie mystérieuse d'Alexandre Dumas fils*, Chronique médicale 1916, p. 392, Cf J. Grasset, *op. cit.* p. 166.

35 K. O. Schmidt, *op. cit.*, p. 44 ff.

36 K. O. Schmidt, *op. cit.*, p. 44 ff.

37 The argument for re-incarnation based on "resemblance" between two people, one of whom is born after the other's death, reveals a complete ignorance of some studies recently published on the question of heredity. Not only strictly physical characteristics (color, shape, size, etc.) may be transmitted by heredity, but also psychic characteristics. To understand this, it is not necessary to resort to materialistic explanations and identify the psychic with the material life. It suffices to refer to the doctrine of Aristotle who declares, like all scholastic philosophers, that the sensorial faculties (sight,

hearing, touch, imagination, memory etc.) are not functions of the soul alone, but of the individual composed substantially of soul and body. As to the "intellectual faculties" (intelligence, will-power), although they are functions of the soul alone, they nevertheless depend essentially, as far as their activity is concerned, on the sensorial faculties and by the way of these on our organic constitution. The parents in begetting the child's body indirectly mould all his psychic faculties.

So, when Mrs. Besant maintains that science asserts that parents do not transmit to their children their psychic characteristics (*The ancient wisdom,* ed. cit., p. 173-174), she is certainly thinking of the teaching of the Sages of the Far East. Mrs. Besant had no confidence in Western Science. Mrs. Blavatsky was responsible for this. According to her, one could notice in all the best modern psychologists their complete inability to explain the nature of intelligence (*The Key to Theosophy,* Point Loma, 1913, p. 88, 122.). But Mrs. Blavatsky's biography sufficiently reveals to us that she never made a thorough study of modern psychology.

38 *Traité méthodique de Science occulte,* Paris, 1891, p. 297. It is in this megalomania that the author finds the main reason why "since 50 years, spiritualism no longer thrives" (*ibid.*) See also Papus (G. A. V. Encausse), *La réincarnation et la métempsychose,* Paris, 1912, p. 138-139.

39 Cf. Tertull., *De Anima,* c. 35; P. L. 2, 697 etc.

40 D. D. Home, *Lights and Shadows of Spiritualism,* New York 1849, p. 281.

41 *Human personality and its survival of bodily death,* New York, London 1897, p. 283.

42 Papus (G.A.V. Encausse) *La réincarnation et la métempsychose,* Paris, 1912, p. 138-139; 142-143.

43 Annie Besant, *La vie occulte de l'homme,* Paris, p. 103. See also W. Lutoslawski, *Niesm. duszy.,* ed. cit., p. 305.

44 Annie Besant, *The paths of discipleship,* 1918 Krotona, p. 63-66.

45 *The Key to Theosophy,* Point Loma, Calif., 1913, pp. 66, 68.

46 *Ibid.*

CHAPTER VI

PARAMNESIA

1. The following argument is often put forward among others in favor of re-incarnation. Someone enters a city he has never seen before in his life, and strangely enough everything seems "familiar" to him[1]; sometimes he feels like telling what he is going to see around the corner of the street[2]. This "impression of having already seen" is very clear with some subjects[3]. It is a fact of experience. But it has to be explained. Now we are told that all explanations given by psychologists are miserable failures. The only satisfactory one, so Camille Flammarion and Irving S. Cooper assert, is found in re-incarnation[4]. Yes, proclaims E. D. Walker, re-incarnation alone can make intelligible to us "the impression of having already seen", as well as the sudden sensation of being very old which sometimes takes hold of us without any plausible reason[5].

2. One cannot deny that the explanation given by the re-incarnationists is very simple. If, on looking at something, you have the impression of having seen it before, it means that you really have already seen it. But if it is impossible for you to have seen it in this life, you must have seen it in another one.

Unfortunately the simplicity of an explanation is not always a proof of its correctness. The re-incarnationists in appealing too swiftly to re-incarnation, clash with the "principle of economy", to which we have already referred. Just as one does not, in practical life, hire a thousand workers to accomplish something which could be done as fast and as well by ten, so in a matter of science, one should not admit any reason able to explain a fact, but choose the one reason which will be strictly "sufficient". This is so because scientific explanation is based on law; and a law implies a necessity. Then a scientific explanation should be sought only in strictly necessary reasons.

On the ground of the "principle of economy", it is not permissible to appeal to causes which belong to another world as long as one has not demonstrated, with complete evidence, the "insufficiency" of those that can be found in this one. Now the reincarnationists do not even take the trouble to look for the explanation of this phenomenon in ordinary psychology. They immediately—and much too quickly— resort to re-incarnation.

3. In order to discover the true explanation let us first state the facts precisely. A man passes by something. He suddenly has the feeling: "I have seen this before." However, he cannot remember where nor when. This inability is not always pleasant, neither is it especially painful; it does not strike us as an abnormal thing. A little thinking, resorting to some mnemonic device, or else the use of hypnosis, are often enough to revive the memory of forgotten details.

The fact which Th. Ribot tells in reference to this is especially enlightening. A man with a very artistic temperament goes on an excursion near the castle of the Earl of Sussex. He approaches the gate, and suddenly he has a vivid impression of having seen it before: moreover, he thinks he has also seen before the persons who are on the road and the donkeys in front of the main entrance. Greatly surprised, he asks his mother for some explanation. She tells him that at the age of 16 months he was taken on an excursion to this same place; that he was carried in a basket on a donkey's back, then left with the donkeys and their guides while the other people who were taking part in the excursion climbed the steps up to the principal entrance.[6]

It also often happens that when investigating this feeling of "having already seen" which overcomes us all of a sudden, we find we did not see exactly the same thing, but something very much like it.

Sometimes also we realize that we have only thought of

that very thing, or one like it; or that we read a book or an article pertaining to it; or we simply heard of it; and sometimes we saw it in a dream. I myself have experienced this on several occasions, beyond any doubt. All of these facts belong in the category of simple errors of memory; they are related to a faulty localization of memories.

4. But there are others which are much more puzzling. Here are some which were observed in the course of a personal investigation. And first this one. One of my students at the university wrote to me: "I am seated at my desk; the door opens and I see one of my comrades who says a few words to me. At the same moment the thought flashes into my mind like lightning that I had once before been in the same situation and the same environment. The picture of my comrade at the door, that of the whole room, the exact terms of the questions were absolutely nothing new to me; I have lived through all of it before."[7] Another person answering our investigation wrote: "During a conversation someone asks a question; I remember perfectly having heard it asked. Another person answers; I have already heard the answer. A third person speaks, and I again think that I have already heard what he says and in identical circumstances. . ." Someone else wrote: "It was during the holidays. I took a walk in the woods. I was looking in the distance. Suddenly something inexpressible happened to me: I felt as if I had been taken back to the past; the act of vision by which I encompassed the panorama of the woods belonged to the past; I was seized with a very sharp and painful anxiety. All this happened like lightning, but it left me quite upset for some time."

The facts which have just been mentioned are classified in psychology under the name of "paramnesia". The characteristic of this phenomenon is the association in the same instant of duration—of present and past; this association is not always perfectly clear, but sometimes it is most impressive.

[64]

PARAMNESIA

Here is the problem offered by paramnesia: how can one and the same psychic act belong at the same time to the present and the past? We have already explained somewhere else that the present and the past constitute two different moments of the same movement. As such they can never meet, they can never share in one and the same reality. They follow each other, that is to say that one appears when the other disappears; the disappearing of the one is the condition sine qua non of the other's appearing. And the principle of contradiction excludes the very possibility of their coexistence. All this shows us that in paramnesia there cannot be any question of that return of time to which some re-incarnationists allude. One can only wonder how to explain the encounter of the feeling of the present with the feeling of the past. This is the way the problem should be stated.

Various hypotheses have been proposed as a solution[8]. We cannot discuss them in detail. We shall limit ourselves to mentioning the two arguments which have been thought to combat those of the re-incarnationists. René Guenon explains paramnesia by "ancestral memory": what a person sees in the present with the effective color of memory had been seen by one of his ancestors[9]. This point of view is inadmissible! First, because it would be impossible to prove that any one ancestor of one of three persons in the case which was studied above, may really have seen the mentioned objects. Moreover, the theory takes it for granted (and it is not so) that memory may be inherited. The author of that thesis confuses the faculty of remembering past facts with the content of the act of memory. The faculty is based on the cerebral organ which the child receives at birth from his parents. Here we can speak of heredity. But the content of memory, the details of the facts which are registered by it, are not transmitted to descendants[10]. "The careful observations of all those who have had to bring up the children of criminals, or children with a tainted heredity," says J. Chevalier, "prove that these children, providing that they are taken in their infancy, do not show a morality inferior to the average."[11]. "Neither science nor virtue are hereditary"[12]. A Chinese child brought soon after his birth to the United States will learn English as well as any other children. He will not display any special facility for the Chinese language.

Philosophy corroborates the conclusions of experience. Whatever way we may explain memory, it always supposes the existence of a kind of psychic image which remains in the subject after consciousness of the perception has vanished. It is therefore an intransmissible characteristic of the subject. It is only the subject who has formerly "known" the thing who can "recognize" it. This is why R. Guenon's opinion is indefensible. Baumann strives to explain the phenomenon of paramnesia in a different way: It appears, he says, when any group of perceptions awakes in us a strong feeling of familiarity with the object, and this feeling is due to the fact that, more or less consciously, we have often thought of it[13]. This hypothesis is no more admissible than the preceding one. It might explain some "amnesias" mentioned above, but not paramnesia properly so called. Moreover, if the fact of having often thought of a certain thing were sufficient to cause paramnesia, it would occur more frequently and in all individuals. Finally, whatever is agreeable to us may produce the feeling of familiarity with it; but this feeling is certainly very different from that which accompanies a well specified case of paramnesia.

Let us now present the positive explanation of the fact. We will first observe that the phenomenon of paramnesia is relatively rare. After our investigation, we have even been inclined to conclude that it appears only in more or less sick persons; this peculiarity has repeatedly been pointed out by our subjects themselves. The sickness blamed for it was, generally, neurasthenia, or psychasthenia.

In order to understand the mechanism by which these mentioned affections may produce the phenomenon of paramnesia, we must briefly explain first the mnemonic process, that is to say, the way in which memory grasps the past. It does not grasp it in itself. For the past in itself does not exist in the order of reality. It can be grasped only by means of the "traces" left in ourselves, that is, by means of the image that formerly made an impression on our consciousness.

This image should not be conceived of as a "static" being, that is to say, as a state of the subject, but as a "dynamic" being, as an act, or if preferred, a movement. In the contrary case, it would necessarily give us the impression of a thing of the present; it would never give us the impression of the past.

But that is not enough: for the "present" is not a passive condition either, but an action. Now the image of the past is "movement" also in another sense. Our psychic life is not a motionless nunc stans; it is a flux; our perceptions, our thoughts, our desires, our feelings flow constantly. We are aware of this motion for the same reason as of the single perceptions which constitute it. The perception of a past psychic fact is carried out precisely in this form because we perceive it according to the perspective of this motion. As we judge the distance of an object in space by looking successively at the whole series of objects which separate us from it, so do we appreciate the "past" of a psychic fact by going over more or less unconsciously, all this dynamic perspective of which it is one of the elements. It follows that any actual perception, if we only encircle it in this dynamic flow, will easily assume an aspect of the "past".

What we have just said hardly seems open to question. One may only wonder what the factors are which can, so to speak, remove the psychic fact from the present and place it in the flux of past psychic facts. It is extremely probable that this can happen only under the influence of illness, since people who are subject to paramnesia are not in good health. However, all ailments do not render people subject to paramnesia in the same degree. A certain nervous or psychic weakness, chronic or temporary, is necessary. If we are right in our observations, the two closely related ailments would be neurasthenia and psychasthenia.

We cannot here describe them in detail. They have already been studied at length by several psychologists, especially by Peter Janet. One remark will be sufficient. These illnesses utterly upset the affective life. This symptom is especially evident in several forms of psychasthenia: those who are affected with it suffer from a kind of deep discontent and chronic depression. Spinoza had already observed and rightly that "sadness" (he uses the word in the broadest sense) lessens action in us. This brings with it a weakening of the sense of our personality, from which comes the impression of debility and that chronic irritation which shows itself in absurd actions and different phobias. All our affections and perceptions begin to assume a general character of strangeness and unreality; they lack the freshness and fulness of the conscious life of the healthy individual.

The obsession (fixed idea) itself, which often accompanies this kind of disease is, in our opinion, the consequence of this peculiar affective state; it is the secondary or derived symptom of it. This is why the fundamental function of the mind remains untouched; in spite of all the morbid symptoms, the judgment generally remains sound; the subject is aware of all his own absurdities and condemns them; and his intellectual productivity may sometimes surpass that of people in perfect health.

We can now better understand why a psychasthenic is especially subject to attacks of paramnesia. The characteristics of paramnesia, as we know, consist in looking at the present according to the "perspective of the past". The psychasthenic does not sense, in his acts, the plenitude of the present. At times (after a process the details of which are very difficult to grasp) this specific deficiency takes the form of an attack of paramnesia. Intelligence (which remains intact with the psychasthenic) very quickly corrects this wrong impression. That is why it lasts only an instant; it is a kind of "distraction".

Among the "distractions" of this type, one must place "the impression of old age" which some people sometimes feel most vividly. This is not a question of a feeling of fatigue, which is a consequence of physiological or psychological old age. It is a question of sudden crises which stir the soul to its very depth and make one suddenly believe that one has lived a long, a very long time. . . .

In fact, these crises which come like lightning, as people tell us who are their victims, create in them a strange personality, scattered and singularly elusive; a personality which lacks, one might say, the clear contours by which it could differentiate itself from other things, while the fire of its interior dynamism, of its own life, dies out. Such is the extremely painful feeling which takes hold of patients of this second class.

Fortunately, it passes quickly, as quickly as lightning. Lightning or obscuring? We very soon recover full self-consciousness, they say; a more vivid feeling of our own strength, our own action and individuality. This "impression of old age" is a classical symptom of psychasthenia, an affliction more frequent than one thinks it to be. As we see, it does not prove anything in favor of re-incarnation.

[1] Camille Flammarion, *La Mort et son Mystère III: Après la Mort,* Paris, p. 436.

[2] Irv. S. Cooper, *op. cit.,* p. 82.

[3] Camille Flammarion, *op. cit.,* p. 436.

[4] Camille Flammarion, *l. c.,* Irv. S. Cooper, *l. c.*

[5] *Re-incarnation, A study of forgotten truth,* London, 1888, p. 20.

[6] Cf. G. Dumas, *Traité de Psychologie,* t. II, Paris, 1924, p. 712.

[7] March 11, 1934.

[8] H. Bergson, Th. Ribot, Pierre Janet, W. James, Dromard et Albes, etc.

[9] *L'Erreur Spirite,* Paris, 1923, pp. 249-250.

[10] This is discussed in detail in *Psychol, Metaph.,* Rome, 1948, p. 469 suiv.

[11] *L'Habitude,* Paris, 1929, p. 129.

[12] J. Chevalier, *l. c.,* p. 130.

[13] *Elemente der Philos.* p. 190, Cf. E. Zeller, *Die Philos. der Griechen,* t. I, VI Aufl., p. 38).

CHAPTER VII

VIRTUAL MEMORY

1. The argument appealed to by the advocates of re-incarnation in order to show that the memory of our past lives exists in us is devoid of any convincing strength. The most enlightened of re-incarnationists are fully conscious of this. And, as they appreciate the value of the objections presented to them[1], they constantly resort to new reasons.

Whatever the nature of formal memory may be, they reply, there is in all of us, in every way and without exception, a virtual memory of our past lives. In order to understand what this virtual memory consists of, it is sufficient to consider the following fact of daily experience: we still read correctly today while we remember nothing of the detailed instructions given to us formerly in view of this result. In the same way, we play an instrument with facility without remembering any of the precise rules we had to follow in the beginning in order to acquire a good technique. Again, we would not touch a red-hot iron, although we do not always carry in mind the memory of having burnt ourselves once at an age when we were barely able to walk. In all these cases, our actual experience exists only as a consequence of forgotten tests, of which, however, something remains, a kind of sketch. This is what the re-incarnationists call "virtual memory".

And they hasten to insinuate: But do we not bring with us, when we are born, much of this "virtual memory"? One person is born with a special talent for music, another for painting, still another with a remarkable gift for mathematics, etc. Moreover, everyone shows, almost from his birth, special sympathies or antipathies, either for certain people, or for places and things which he sees for the first time[2]. A great many men possess qualities which are generally only found in women; on the other hand, some women show, in many circumstances, virtues which incontestably belong to manhood. Finally, some people spend their whole lives in futile dreams; all their aspirations constantly leave their capacities far behind. All these phenomena are certainly characteristic manifestations of virtual memory; if someone is born with a special capacity for music, or painting, or science, it is evidently because these talents are not new to him. He has used them in a former life. He acquired this "habit" before being born into this world. If someone we meet for the first time inspires us with deep confidence, or a noble sympathy[3], is it not clear that he is no stranger to us? We had friendly relations with him in a former life. And the antipathy which we feel suddenly for someone else proves also that we face someone who was our enemy in another life. If you experience a phobia which nothing justifies at the sight of a sheet of water, or of a large open space, it is because, in one of your preceding existences, you were drowned, or you were sentenced to be executed in a public square. If you are a man and feel a peculiar attraction for women's occupations, this means that you were a woman in olden times. On the contrary, if you are a woman and give evidence of absolutely virile tastes, it is because one cannot at will free one's self from confirmed habits: you were a man in a past life[4]. Finally there are incorrigible dreamers whose days are devoted only to dreaming, and who seem to suffer from a kind of congenital disproportion between the faculty of wishing and that of acting. What can be the origin of such a lack of harmony in the psychic personality of human beings? The solution is quite simple: dreamers are punished in this way in this world for the lazy life they have led at other times and in other places.

2. What are we to say? First, if on the one hand, we cannot deny that the explanation of the re-incarnationists is a very simple one, we should remember that, on the other hand, simplicity is not always a proof of truth. Moreover, do they

not go too far in simplifying the problem? Secondly, if a theory is to deserve the consideration of scientific minds, it must not limit itself to the realm of mere possibilities. It must necessarily offer some positive reason enabling the mere possibility to be transformed into probability. The argument of the re-incarnationists fails also on that account, as we shall see a little further on. Thirdly, a good method necessitates the explanation of psychological phenomena by psychic forces. This is so by reason of the principle of economy discussed before. Only if we could demonstrate positively that the consideration of the intervention of these forces is not sufficient to explain the phenomenon, would it be permissible to resort to some other explanation. But in order to declare this explanation by psychic forces inadequate, should not we first know them thoroughly? Now, not only do the advocates of re-incarnation scorn "Western psychology" but, they prove moreover that they do not know it. Fourthly, it is inadmissible to apply a primitive mentality to modern scientific research. In order to fully explain what I mean let me tell of an adventure of one of my friends in a village of the High Tatras. He asked the mountaineer who was driving the car, "What do you call this mountain?" And the man scornfully replied: "What? You don't know?" My friend answered sharply: "And you, do you know everything?" And the mountaineer boldly retorted, "Certainly, I know everything." Happy man! He knows everything! For him, there are no problems! Let us not demand that Science explain everything. There are mysteries in Nature. The ideal of Science is to succeed in explaining everything finally, but the ideal can never be reached in this world. The aim of Science will have been reached when all individual problems are reduced to some general problems; when it will have discovered the existing analogies and outlined the proper method to discover the best possible explanation of natural phenomena.

Again, when we speak of "virtual memory", we would do well first to ask ourselves the following question: Is it true that we have forgotten all the details of the lessons we had to learn, writing, playing an instrument, etc.? Do we not remember both the teacher and the school that we went to, and the lessons themselves, as well as a number of details pertaining to this subject? Our present skill as a writer, or a musician, cannot be considered as some heaven-sent capacity; quite the contrary, it is our own work. If it is deeply rooted in our being, it is due to long repeated personal efforts and, after all, thanks to the exercise of our formal memory. But we never possess any such memory of the psychic phenomena which are the subject of the present debate.

We have now reached the last argument and it is of great importance. Are all capacities, all tendencies, all inclinations to which the re-incarnationists refer in this case, really "inborn" in the literal sense of the word? We may, at least, doubt it. For instance, if someone hears from his childhood, a certain art, or a certain science, being praised again and again, he will most probably form a high opinion of that art or that science, which, from then on, will constitute for him a kind of ideal. This ideal once conceived, the child will naturally strive to realize it, and this all the more as a special effort attracts his comrades' attention to him. This first success, which awakens the latent forces of ambition, and concentrates the aspirations and energies of the mind on one aim, prepares the way for further progress and the talent will then reach a remarkable development. There are many people unconscious of their own talents and many genii in a latent state; unfavorable circumstances have not permitted their awakening and their blossoming.

The same thing is true to a certain extent of alleged features of our character, which are often just the results of our education. A man who was brought up exclusively by women and a little too much coddled during his childhood and adolescence, will seem rather effeminate. Finally, many sympathies, antipathies, aversions, phobias, originate in a "traumatic" memory, a memory which the subject has quite often absolutely forgotten. For instance, Theresa Newmann, the famous stigmatized woman of Konnersreuth in Bavaria, has a great aversion for longhaired animals. The reason being that in her childhood some such animal caused her an intensely disagreeable sensation. Descartes, so says Condillac, "always had a liking for squinting eyes because the first person he loved, had this defect"'. Contemporary psychology and psychiatry take account of many similar facts, when the "emotive-shock" (or "actual emotion") long disappeared, leaves behind none-the-less what is called an "emotional state", that is to say, a kind of dynamic tension, something like a certain coloring of psychic life, a particular "mental attitude".

These tendencies of psycho-traumatic origin obey certain specific laws, among which the "law of individuality of instincts" is of great importance. It can be expressed as follows: instinct, as soon as it has found full satisfaction in any object, loses ipso facto its impetus towards all objects of the same kind. Hence our unreasonable liking for certain places and certain persons as if these places, these persons, alone could make us happy. In short, many qualities which at first sight seem "inborn" are really "acquired".

3. There are, however, qualities the existence of which could not be explained in this way. Education often just superficially skims, so to speak, the soul, without penetrating to its depths. Certain temperaments are strangely refractory to the action of external factors, and energetically preserve their own physiognomy. In this way, we have sympathies and antipathies which cannot be explained only by the theory of "traumatic memory". Besides the external factors then, one must admit that in each individual some internal factors intervene, which he possessed at birth. These are the ones which determine his temperament, his inner personality. To ask why Peter has such or such qualities, while Paul has different ones, is the same as asking why Peter is Peter and Paul is Paul. In short, the problem grows and becomes one with the more general problem of the origin of instincts.

4. The advocates of re-incarnation believe that all instincts are but "habits" transmitted by parents to their descendants. This is, obviously, the same idea as that of the evolutionists. Moreover, they do not deny it. The following texts prove this assertion. It is evolution, says Alba, which constitutes one of the main supports of theosophy and, consequently, of the theory of re-incarnation[6]. "Every one of us," states Camille Flammarion, "was an animal before becoming man; but man is not the last step in evolution"[7]. Animals may, after several re-incarnations, appear to us in a human form, J. Ch. Chatterji asserts[8]. "The soul of a musically inclined child may have come from the nightingale, the sweet singer of our woods. A child who shows taste for architecture may have inherited the soul of a beaver, the architect of the woods and waters"[9].

The theory of evolution has already been discussed elsewhere. Here are the conclusions which we reached[10]: evolution, to be logical, must suppose that the first individuals of all species had no instinct. However, this supposition is not only gratuitous but inadmissible. It is gratuitous. What is it based on? On the sole fact that some of the instincts of animals may be slightly modified under the influence of man and circumstances. Now to draw from this single fact such a general conclusion as is expressed by evolutionists, is really to think too little of the fundamental principles of induction. In reality, these modifications are quite superficial, as everyone knows, and no trace of modification so profound as is considered possible by evolutionists, can be found in the history of species. Moreover, it would have to be proved, (which has not yet been done) that the characteristics acquired by individuals (or "individual characteristics") can be inherited. Finally, if instincts originally emerged through evolution alone, why do we not today see new instincts constantly appearing?

But the inference that the first individuals of each species had no instinct—a gratuitous inference, as shown above—

is inacceptable, for animals deprived of any instinct would not have been able to feed or to defend themselves, and consequently they would inevitably have died. Let us notice also that some instincts have only one opportunity to act in the life of the animal, that is when it has laid its egg. Such instincts could not have been transmitted by the parents in the very act of generation! How then could the instincts of the worker bees ever have been transmitted, since the workers do not lay eggs?

The living being certainly had to possess from the beginning some tendencies, some characteristics, as well as a certain organism which is his own, a certain typical structure. And these tendencies are not added to the organism by chance. On the contrary, they are an inseparable and integral part of its "dynamic structure". But this point has been discussed[11].

The following example will illustrate it in a concrete way: why does the bird build his nest only when spring is near?[12] It is easily explained: as spring is coming (with changing climatic conditions) a deep modification occurs in the bird's organism, starting the physiological process which results in an increase of endocrinal secretions, an activation of the production of hormones etc. All of this reacts on the sensitive system of the bird through variations of blood pressure, of internal temperature, of similar influences, thus exciting special desires which normally develop into external activity.

Thus the actions of the bird at the new season are the result of certain desires, coming from sensations which ultimately depend on elementary physiological transformations. There is no room here for any anomaly, any exception to the laws which rule the functioning of the organism. A given sensation always brings a determined reaction. In the animal deprived of free will, any desire necessarily becomes an action, a movement.

And this is why the bird can build his nest without having any pre-existing image of the nest to coordinate his movements when building it. Certain experiences really seem to prove that animals never have such images. If, for instance, one makes a hole in one of the cells of a honeycomb, the bee will continue to put honey in. It will never think of a necessary repair. On the other hand, it knows how to get over the difficulties and avoid the obstacles it encounters in the course of its work. It is conscious of its movements only. In the same way, if the bird builds his nest skillfully, it is not thanks to a complete image which guided him in his work, but thanks to that peculiar and harmonious structure of his physiological individuality which, at the right moment, adequately coordinates all his movements. Our theory of instinct is based on a certain finality in nature which expresses and asserts itself in the harmonious structure of the living organisms.

But we must answer an objection which will no doubt be raised. There are, it will be said, birds of slightly different species whose organisms are very much alike and which nevertheless have different instincts. One species will build quite different nests from another. Does not this fact contradict our theory which seems to make the nature of instinct dependent on the structure of the organism? Should not the instincts resemble each other when the birds have similar organisms? This argument seems to ignore the difference between an ordinary machine and a precision machine. To disturb the functioning of an ordinary machine to a noticeable degree, it takes something important. But a little thing is enough to disturb the functioning of a precision machine. And the organism is a precision machine. This is why the least drop of venom, a trifling quantity of poison, is sometimes sufficient to call forth in a man's mind absolutely new tendencies, or to completely modify his way of thinking and feeling; even sometimes to cause a serious mental disorder. Why wonder then that an imperceptible modification in the structure of an organism may create particular instincts, which remain unknown to birds of similar species?

5. We have only appealed to this argument to explain the origin of the "specific" instincts. But, it also makes clear the genesis of the "individual" instincts. Let us suppose that an individual has in his organism certain biological capacities which vary according to the physical conditions of his environment, that is to say depending on the circumstances of his generation, and his evolution, on climate, on his hereditary tendencies, etc. The combination of all these influences will give the specific inclinations of this individual a special physiognomy, will determine the character of all his "individual" instincts. Just as the peculiarities of the diabetic's organism move him to drink water to excess, another organism will be unable to take a great quantity of liquids; there are individuals and even whole families who are more or less affected with hydrophobia, and this for natural reasons well known to the doctor. "Hydrophobia" does not necessarily come from a "drowning" undergone in some previous life, as claimed by the re-incarnationists. And the same is true of other "phobias". But, most of the time, they are only characteristic symptoms of diverse nervous deficiencies, such as neurasthenia and psychasthenia. These symptoms, in their turn, are the consequences of deep organic changes.

6. To the number of these "individual" instincts one should also add the unaccountable feeling of sympathy which sometimes rises in us at the sight of a person whom we meet for the first time. When it is a question of sexual sympathy ("sex appeal") this is so obvious, that the believers in reincarnation give up arguing. They merely maintain that "nobler" sympathies can only be explained by the fact of a former existence in which the two individuals freely exchanged their thoughts and feelings, so that their actual sympathy is the consequence of old habits, acquired in another life when they lived near each other.

We believe, on the contrary, that spontaneous sympathies possessing the character of noble friendship, also belong in the category of instincts. In order to understand this, it is enough to remember that in the soul of every man, there is his ideal, in the broadest sense of this word. But, from a psychological point of view, aspiration towards an ideal is a kind of nostalgia, the object of which is the fulfilment of our own capacities or the perfecting of our whole being. This explains the apparently disconcerting fact, that the ideal which seems to dwell in inaccessible regions and always infinitely surpass us, is, however, always so near to us, so familiar, and always shows us a kind and fraternal face. The ideal is to us like an old friend. This should not surprise us, for the ideal is our creation; it is the refrain our soul sings, it is the animating force of our own spiritual being. Thus understood, the ideal takes diverse forms, sometimes even rather unexpected ones. I once asked a child of Cracovia, "What will you do later?" He answered "I want to be a blacksmith." "That is a beautiful trade." The child's face became gloomy: "No," he explained, "I shall be a blacksmith because my father wants me to. I want to be something quite different." Then, he added, in a low voice as if fearing to be overheard: "Oh! how I would like to be a chimney-sweep!" "Why?" And the child answered: "Because I love to walk on the roofs!" At that time, this was the only ideal of this urchin.

According to his own psychic constitution, each of us pictures to himself (more or less consciously and quite often unconsciously) an image of the ideal companion. Now the people we meet on our way answer to this ideal in rather different degrees. This is why not everyone in our entourage can become a friend. There will always be persons who, in spite of all our regard for them, will never inspire our hearts with that feeling of familiarity and confidence which a friend gives us; we shall always find their presence somewhat boring and tiring.

To ask why one person is sympathetic to us and another

indifferent, is somewhat like asking why all foods do not taste alike. The same individual may be sympathetic to one person and antipathetic to another. The caprices of nature are not limited to gastronomy! Is it necessary to add that these caprices manifest themselves most in persons who have never learned to discipline their desires? In order to explain sympathy and antipathy, which are natural manifestations, there is no need to appeal to the fantastic suggestions of the re-incarnationists.

7. The believers in re-incarnation also say: there are people whose aspirations surpass by far their physical capacities to realize them. These persons dream of great things which evidently are out of their reach, they strive towards lofty aims, which they will never attain. Where is the key to this mystery? Re-incarnation: If some one did not know how to turn his talent to account in one of his previous existences, it will be sterile in the course of following lives.

It is enough to understand fully the psychological nature of what is called "aspiration" to see the whole arbitrary character of this reply. Aspirations is just another name for the wishes and tendencies which stir the human being; it is the will in the widest sense of this word.

But what is will? It is an immanent reaction of the subject to an agitation of consciousness caused by a group of exterior incitements or accompanying representations; it is a dynamic attitude which he adopts towards this group. If the object seems good to him, the subject answers by love; if it seems bad, he answers by aversion; if it seems neither good nor bad, his response is indifference. All knowledge, whatever its nature may be, spontaneously calls forth in us a certain reaction which normally becomes a tendency, the full satisfaction of which would be the real union of the subject with the loved object, or his separation from that hated object.

In order to repress unpleasant results which might come from such reactions, it will often be necessary to oppose the first act of knowledge which produced them with another which is automatically followed by another contrary reaction. Sometimes this opposition takes place without any effort on the part of the subject: an image suddenly affects our senses by its very brilliant color, but another image suddenly engrosses our attention, diverts our former thoughts, and annihilates the dynamic reaction which was stirred up by the first perception. When a wolf sees a sheep, he is ready to jump on it; but when he hears the shepherd's voice, he leaves the sheep and runs away.

In man, the balance between the two antagonistic reactions may come in yet another way. Thanks to an understanding which is his privilege, he appreciates the good, not only in the present but also in the future, by the vision he forms of all the unfortunate consequences which might follow that present good. Now the vision of these future consequences may have such a strong influence on him that the present good has no longer any attraction. Not only can this paralyze the action of the subject, but also certain thoughts concerning the present good. In fact, since man has the power of abstraction, he is able to bring out the essential characters of good, of good in itself; of ideal and perfect good. Once he has excluded from his ideal good any bad element, his will tends with all its force toward this good. He is quite free not to think of it. But when he does think of it, he cannot lose his interest in it. This good constitutes the end of the aspirations of his will, so much so that all other particular goods interest him only in so far as they bear the stamp of this ideal good.

It goes without saying that no terrestrial good is susceptible of fully satisfying such a love. In any pleasure, any wealth, any glory, human reason will not be long in discovering some imperfection, which will make them less desirable. And this is why man's character always makes him want to rise higher and higher, never to be satisfied with present gratifications. In this respect we are all "dreamers" and it is only natural. On the contrary, man would become really abnormal if he could fully realize his happiness in the present. He would then be like children and animals!

But is there a single faculty in us which is not threatened by degeneration? Even dreams, this noble privilege of our nature, may be wrong and lead us astray. They ought to be the wings which carry us to the zenith; yet, often, they are but a weight which fastens us down. Some are so absorbed in the contemplation of their ideal that they gradually lose all contact with the world, end by living entirely on illusions, and thus make out of a power of thought which might be active and fruitful, a somber reverie without any profit or aim.

This kind of disorder may have diverse causes: lack of experience for some, lack of spiritual discipline for others; but, most of the time, it is caused simply by lack of will power (aboulia). For lack of experience many people do not realize what is possible and what impossible; they undertake a thousand things which they have to give up right away. Others, for want of disciplining their minds, do not know enough to stop dreaming, to no purpose, wonderful and futile dreams.

More or less, we are all prone to "solitary monologues", we like to tell ourselves all kinds of stories which to us are all the more agreeable because in them we always act a beautiful part. These dreams pursue even those who work steadily. They constitute the poetry of our life; they are as it were its necessary complement. Such colloquies do not in themselves reveal anything abnormal. However, in persons suffering from "aboulia" (whatever its origin may be) they sometimes take a hypertrophic form. Many people go to psychiatrists to ask them for a cure from importunate "dreams" which prevent them from working or sleeping. Sometimes a trifle is enough to start an uninterrupted parade of images which they cannot stop. Unable to pin their attention on any task, they even often become unable to understand what they read or what they are told. Their thinking becomes confused;

they find it more and more difficult to make decisions; finally, discouraged, they renounce useful work, estrange themselves from the real world and seclude themselves in the world of dreams as in a kind of fourth dimension: the land of "aboulia", dreams. Under the impression that they are governed by their own thoughts, they often come to the conclusion that these are imposed on them by a stranger, that they are chased by a malevolent person, "possessed by the devil". Others again describe their torment as a "flight of thoughts": somebody is stealing their ideas away from them! No doubt all these symptoms are not equally strong in all subjects. "Aboulia" may assume the most varied forms. This dreaming and these sterile aspirations offer a whole scale of shades and degrees. But whatever form they take, they could not be considered as providing any argument whatever in favor of re-incarnation. They are but the symptoms of a well defined, well known disease.

8. We must say a word about a last problem: that of genius. One knows with what eagerness the advocates of re-incarnation seize upon this case to support their theory. Whatever one may think about "aspirations", so they say, it is certain that "genius" can never be explained by the laws of psychology. " Psychological laws" are only a generalization of some psychic process which we may observe daily around us. Now genius has an exceptional, even an extraordinary character; therefore one cannot bring it under general rules. A man who is a genius has neither father nor mother, nor posterity of his own kind. His parents have not usually shown themselves to be extraordinary beings; his descendants do not, as a rule, rise above mediocrity. The man of genius all of a sudden rises far above his family; he dazzles men and disappears without leaving anything of his own nature behind. Genius cannot be transmitted by heritage.

In view of this unique case, official science remains silent, declare the re-incarnationists. Our theory alone gives the clue to the enigma. The soul of a genius is very old and has already had a long series of re-incarnations[13]; it has had time to collect many experiences. And its special superiority over other souls is due precisely to these experiences.

Before passing on to a positive psychological explanation of the case, we should notice that many of the reproduced affirmations quoted should be verified. They are far from being as evident as they would like to make us believe. For instance, what is the basis of the following: genius has no parents and no descendants? It cannot be a question here of the very "idea" of genius; otherwise it is a vicious circle! Neither is it based on facts of experience, these being, in most cases, impossible to verify. For instance, how could one ascertain that the genius of Pasteur did not proceed from his ancestry? But did Pasteur's father, a simple workman, ever have the opportunity to reveal his genius, if he had any? Many other men of genius are in the same case. On the other hand, how could it be proved by experience that genius is always without descendants[14]? A great many people of genius did not found a family: Thomas Aquinas, Anselm, Suarez, Scott, Descartes, Malebranche, Spinoza, Leibnitz, Hume, Kant, Schopenhauer, A. Comte etc. Many men acknowledged as geniuses have, to be sure, had children of their own. But let us not forget that the psychic personality of the child does not depend on the father alone; it also depends on the mother. The theory of the "spermatists" (formerly sustained by Gallien, Hertsocker, Boerhaave, Leewenhook and others)[15], according to which the germ is contained in the virile element alone, is outdated. Moreover, many scientists even maintain that in a generation resemblance passes from one sex to the other, from the father to the daughter, from the mother to the son, and not from the father to the son and from the mother to the daughter. This fact, if it were proved, would complicate matters still more.

Finally, the very conception of genius that the re-incarnationists have, does not seem to correspond to reality. They seem to think that a genius has, so to speak, nothing in common with the rest of humanity; that he is "essentially" different; that he is a being apart from others, sui generis. According to them, the inventions and all the ideas of genius are the result of sudden intuitions which cross the mind like so many flashes of lightning, and could not have been prepared at all.

Th. Ribot has protested against these conceptions and has said that one should ignore them even when men of genius declare them to be well founded[16]. A. Rey declares that the alleged instantaneousness of creative inspiration is but an illusion. In fact, the appearance of a new idea in the field of consciousness is normally preceded by a long period of more or less conscious elaboration, which might be called the period of incubation. Invention is the result of a steady effort (even though unknown to us) to which our will applies itself in a certain well-determined sense, and which, in the long run, gives birth to that idea which is called genius. Moreover, let us not forget that the appearance of the first idea which puts us on the trail of an invention, is not the invention itself. One must be able to shape the first idea, in other words, to probe and develop it; and this supposes another effort of attention concentrated on such or such a given problem[17].

It is on the strength of this fact that Helvetius calls genius "a steady attention", and Buffon, "a long patience". Cuvier accepts their definitions, for he also says: "Genius is but the patience of common sense." Chesterfield, in his turn, is of the opinion that the faculty of fastening one's attention steadily on one object alone and eliminating any diversion, is the method genius usually follows[18].

These assertions are perhaps a little too absolute. If taken literally, the subjects most affected from the psychopathological point of view, the victims of "obsession", would be the greatest geniuses. A normal person can fasten his attention constantly on one object only if this object can again and again present new aspects; and this is so true that one condition of steady attention is precisely the possibility of continuing to discover in the object different and always new phases.

Therefore one cannot simply identify genius with attention. But the genius, in the most complete sense of this expression, the productive and creative genius, must possess firm will-power, be able—whether by strength of an immanent virtue, or by reason of accidental morbid predispositions —to turn the whole of his mind's activity in a determined direction; to concentrate his attention[19] on all the most diverse aspects of his object. In order to fully perceive all its multiple aspects, he must have a synthetic mind, open and free; not burdened with futile details by a faithful and over-particular memory. He must also have acute curiosity and a special ingenuousness which, in daily life, might easily seem queer and even eccentric. Finally, he must know how to make skillful use of all combinations, substitutions, associations, dissociations, comparisons, and syntheses, to which the ideas lend themselves.

Very often those incitements most susceptible of sustaining such an effort emerge from the very environment, from the petty incidents of common life, incessantly presenting to the mind new problems to solve, stimulating its natural curiosity; inciting it to reasoned imitation by means of that mighty stimulus called emulation. And this at the same time explains why geniuses generally appear not separately, but "in groups"[20].

G. Seailles said with good reason that the laws of genius do not differ from those of psychological life. Between the "genius" and the ordinary talented man, there is no essential difference[21]. The theory which recognizes in the man of genius an "aged soul", a soul for a long time engaged in a kind of pilgrimage through successive re-incarnations, is devoid of any scientific basis. Thus falls the last defense of the partisans of re-incarnations.

9. Before we conclude this chapter we will examine briefly the argument which, for many centuries, has been the favorite

weapon of the believers in re-incarnation in the Western world. It is derived from the "reminiscences". It was set forth by Plato with poetry, logic and psychology.

Our "science", this philosopher says through the mouth of Socrates[22], is in the main only a reminiscence of things we knew before. That is why, when the child begins to learn the first elements of science, he really does not learn anything new. He only recalls the notions of a science which he possessed before he came to this world. Do you want a proof of this? Plato adds. Nothing easier. Ask a person who has never studied, a few questions. If you set about it skillfully, you will easily get excellent answers.

In the dialogue named Meno, Plato presents a special list of questions, by which Socrates supposedly showed his friend Meno "that what we call knowledge is only reminiscence"[23]. Here is the passage:

Socrates (to Meno): Call one of the many servants who accompany you, anyone of them, so that I can show you what you wish to know.

Meno: Wonderful! (To one of his slaves) Come here!

Socrates (to Meno): Be careful; see whether he seems to remember, or to learn from me.

Meno: I will be careful.

Socrates (to the slave): Listen, my friend, do you know that this space is square[24]?

The slave: Yes.

Socrates: And that in a square space these four lines (sides) are equal?

The slave: No doubt.

Socrates: And that these lines which cross it in the middle diagonally are also equal.

The slave: Yes.

Socrates: Can such a space be either smaller or larger?

The slave: Certainly.

Socrates: If this side were two feet long and that other also two, what would the dimension of the whole be? Look at the

thing like this: if there were on this side two feet, and on that
only one, is it not true that the space would be two feet?
The slave: Yes.
Socrates: But when there are also two feet for the second
side, does it not make twice two?
The Slave: Certainly.
Socrates: Now the space is twice two feet?
The slave: Yes.
Socrates: How much is twice two feet? Reckon it yourself
and tell me.
The slave: Four, Socrates.
Socrates: Would it not be possible to have another space
twice the size of this one, but like this one, and also with all
its lines equal?
The slave: Yes. . . .

Socrates asks some more questions and then turns to his
friend: "You see, Meno, that I do not teach him anything:
I restrict myself to questioning him." "Quite so," replies
Meno surprised. "He found out all this by himself."[25] Thus,
independently of studying (this slave has never studied)[26],
Socrates continues, each one of us possesses many ideas in a
latent state. They have not been drawn from the teachings of
this life[27]. They are born in us. They must have been taught
us in a former life.

10. Saint Augustine passed severe judgment on this argument of Plato's. If Plato, he says, was able to get such correct answers from a man without education, it was due only
to the fact that he suggested them by the manner in which he
was questioning him. "All the while the slave was being
asked graduated and logical questions, he realized what was
suggested and told what he had seen"[28]. If the good answers
obtained from the slave really proved a "knowledge of mathematics" which the slave had possessed in a former life, adds
St. Augustine, one would have to suppose that all men without
exception, or nearly so, were formerly mathematicians, for
all men, or nearly all, are able to answer satisfactorily Soc-

rates' questions. And this supposition is absolutely improbable. In fact, "mathematicians are so scarce, that it is rare to meet one"[29].

With regard to this matter, here is another observation of great importance: Socrates could, by way of his "mid-wife method" (as he himself called it), get from his subject only those truths which intelligence sees "in the incorporeal light just as the eye sees color"[30], that is to say truths that one may arrive at by way of analytic judgments. He was never able by such a method to discover in the slave's mind any trace of a fact pertaining to a former life[31].

---

[1] "If there are no memories of the past . . . then most certainly re-incarnation is meaningless and the whole process of evolution a cruel and futile torment" (Irving S. Cooper, *Reincarnation the hope of the world*, Krotona, 1920, pp. 71-72).

[2] "In our opinion, it is impossible to explain otherwise these inborn capacities," says L. Figuier, *Le lendemain de la mort*, 10 ème éd., Paris, 1894, p. 306. Cf. p. 330-332, 340-348, 376-377. Cf. also Allan Kardec, *Le livre des esprits, Paris*, (sans date), pp. 101, 103, 106.

[3] When it is a question of sensual sympathies, even the re-incarnationists are sceptical.

[4] This opinion is rather common among the re-incarnationists. According to them the human being is re-incarnated alternatively in both sexes in order to acquire the plenitude of "human" perfection. Cf. Allan Kardec, *Le livre des esprits*, Paris, sans date, p. 88. J. G. Chatterji, *Philosophie ésotérique de l'Inde*, Paris, 1909, p. 76; Irv. S. Cooper, *Reincarnation the hope of the world*, Krotona, 1920 p. 15; K. O. Schmidt, *op. cit.* pp. 17-18.

[5] *De L'art de penser*, chap. V.

[6] *O celu zycia*, Warszawa, 1926, p. 6.

[7] Camille Flammarion, *La Mort et son Mystère*, III: (*Après la Mort*, p. 430).

[8] *La philosophie ésotérique de l'Inde,* Paris 1909, Ve éd., pp. 65-66.

[9] *The to-morrow of death*, Boston, 1888, p. 247.

[10] *Psychologia Metaphysica*, Romae, 1948, pp. 170-171. *Transformismo Antropologico*, Univ. Cat., Sao Paulo, 1945.

[11] *La psychophysique humaine d'après Aristotle*, Paris, 1930.

[12] Cf. our book *Psych. Metaph.*, Roma, 1948, pp. 173-176.

[13] See Annie Besant, *The necessity of re-incarnation*, London, 1905, pp. 72-76.

[14] "Genius—it is becoming almost a commonplace in science—genius is sterile" (Annie Besant, *The necessity of re-incarnation*, London, 1905, p. 12).

[15] Cf. Th. Ribot, *L'hérédité psychologique*, p. 206.

[16] Cf. Th. Ribot, *Essais sur l'imagination créatrice*, éd. III, Paris, 1908, p. 45 ff.

[17] A. Rey, *Invention artistique, scientifique, pratique;* G. Dumas, *Traité de Psychologie*, t. II, 1924, p. 433.

[18] Cf. W. James, *Principles of psychology*, London, (without date), Vol. I, pp. 423, 421 422. Vol. II, pp. 360-361. The assertion that all true "inventions", whether artistic, literary or scientific are often discovered in sleep, contains a great illusion, as proved by certain concrete examples (H. Bergson, *L'Energie spirituelle: Le Rêve*, Paris, 1924, pp. 99 ff.)

[19] Alienists have long ago observed that people affected by mental disorders have only the power of "spontaneous attention"; their "voluntary attention" is very weak.

[20] Cf. A. Rey, *l. c.*, p. 457.

[21] Cf. A. Rey, *l. c.*, p. 457.

[22] Phaedo, 72 E et suiv.

[23] Meno, 81 E.

[24] While speaking, Socrates was drawing the figures in question on the ground or elsewhere.—Meno, 82A-85B.

[25] Ibid., 85 B.

[26] *Ibid.*, 85 E.

[27] *Ibid.*, 85 E.

[28] *De Trinit.* lib. XII, c. 15; P. L. 42, 1011. See Aristotle, *Anal. Post.* I, 1, 71 a 29 b 7; St. Thomas Aquinas, *S. Theol.*, I, q. 84 a 4.

[29] St. Augustine, *l. c.*

[30] St. Augustine, *l. c.*

[31] Plato deduces the theory of re-incarnation also from the "law of contraries". Here is how Plato expressed this law: "When a thing becomes larger, does it not necessarily imply that it was smaller before growing larger"?—so reasons Socrates. "Yes," replies his listener. "Is it not true"—so Socrates continues—"that when it becomes smaller, it means that a former state in which it was larger must subsequently have given birth to a state in which it is smaller"? "That is right," Socrates' friend answers—"And certainly"—Socrates continues—"what is weaker comes to life from what is stronger, and what is quicker from what is slower?—What more? If anything becomes worse, does it not come from something better? A just thing from an unjust one? That is enough? We maintain this general principle for any generation, that opposite things generate others opposite to themselves." (Phaedo, 70 E—71 A).

Thus, according to Plato "the law of contraries" is a fundamental law of Nature. But, if this were the case, a living being could only come from a dead one, since this represents "the opposite of life." (Phaedo 71 C-D).

It is rather surprising to see philosophers so easily misled by metaphors and believing that simple comparisons are sufficient to explain objective reality. To be satisfied with hasty analogies is most misleading. Let it first be made clear that "the principle of contraries" applies at the very most to homogeneous realities: a greater length presupposes a smaller one; a greater weight presupposes the existence of a smaller weight; the idea of a longer time implies that of a shorter time, which would be included in the first one, etc. But the "principle of the contraries" has no meaning as soon as we face heterogeneous realities; for it is impossible to make a greater length out of a smaller weight, or a longer time out of a smaller density! This fact is self-evident and does not call for further explanation. Now, between life and death there is a difference of the same nature as between length and weight, for instance: a difference in essence, a specific difference.

One can say almost the same thing about the Buddhist law: "Spring gives birth to Winter. Winter gives birth to Spring". Only "oriental mentality", of which we have spoken above, perceives in this statement the shadow of argument. In fact, what is Spring? A substantial being which would be, under certain conditions, susceptible of changing into another one, Winter? Certainly not. The Buddhist saying: "The spring gives birth to winter. . ." is a simple image meant to suggest the unavoidable succession of these two seasons, and not a connection between cause and effect. This aphorism means: "After spring comes the winter. . ." and nothing more.

In Nature we discover no phenomenon presenting a real analogy with reincarnation. The seed thrown into the earth develops into a bud, a stem, a tree; this will live for a time; then it will die; the wind will scatter its decayed wood through the fields, thus fertilizing the soil and aiding the germination of new seeds. But one has never seen, nor ever heard of, decayed wood turning into seed and thus beginning a new series of metamorphosis.

It is true that before changing into decayed wood, the tree produced fruit, the scattered pits of which will in their turn generate new trees; that these will also yield fruit, and so on, indefinitely. But these new trees are not merely a repetition of their ancestors, one of their "re-incarnations"; physically they are not particles of them; they constitute entirely different individuals, substantially distinct units; each one of them has in its structure a plan of organization of its own; seeks, in its evolution, only one object (the welfare of its whole being); in a word, it materializes a unique and singular tendency. And, if one should object that these new trees will always retain a likeness to the primitive tree to which they owe their existence, we shall reply that the result always necessarily has some resemblance to its cause, especially when it derives from it by way of generation, that is to say, by a simple communication of its being. But resemblance does not mean identity.

PART III

THE RE-INCARNATION
IN THE LIGHT OF MORALITY

To judge of re-incarnation from the moral viewpoint, it is advisable that we should refer to Theosophy, because it is only in Theosophy that the moral consequences of this Creed are clearly seen. In other re-incarnationist systems they are considerably modified through the influence of certain dogmas of Christian doctrine, especially by that of "grace". This dogma does not concur with the conception of "immanent justice" which led the Sages of the Extreme Orient to conceive of re-incarnation. For "immanent justice" really requires that atonement for a fault committed should be imposed on the culprit himself and on him alone; it cannot, in any way, be reconciled with the redemptive atonement which the dogma of Grace teaches*.

---

*Jerome A. Anderson, *Re-incarnation, a study of the human soul,* S. Francisco, 1896, pp. 170-175.

CHAPTER I

SALVATION

1. According to the formal teaching of the theosophists man is not a "creature" of God[1]. He is a "fragment of Divinity"[2], "a spark of the Divine"[3], "an offspring of God"[4]. "The nature of God and of man is identical"[5]. "We are the divine will, one with God in our essential being"[6]. "Here is nothing but God everywhere. Nothing but God in all the multiplicity of forms. All thought, all consciousness are His, for He is the One, the only, the eternal Life"[7]. The Divinity of man is the one fundamental truth taught by the Theosophists; the living Divinity in us, they say, is no illusion, but a perfect and indestructible reality[8].

2. This conception of human nature enables us to understand the true meaning of our earthly life. The earthly life of man will no longer be "the service of God" by means of which we may realize the divine will. "Life is a process by which we free God in us"[9]. "We come to this earth"—so Theosophy emphatically asserts—"not in order to avoid the danger of eternal punishment nor to deserve an eternity of bliss, but to release God who is in us"[10]. "You must develop the God within yourself", says the celebrated lady-president of the Theosophical Society[11].

How is man to attain this moral aim? It is evident that he cannot do so by means of an intervention of "Divine Grace". Such a way of looking at things would imply a contradiction. God would give man His "grace", that is to say a very special power, so that man might "release" Him. Hence we can understand why this word "grace" so much disturbs the Theosophists. The dogma of grace is the stumbling block of their theory, because it is opposed to their

conception of Divinity. For indeed the idea of "grace" is in-
dissolubly connected with that of divine free will. And that
divine free will remains incompatible with the pantheistic
philosophy of Theosophists[12]. We have fully explained this
special question in another work[13].

As the God of the pantheists has no free will, He cannot
make a choice; He may not portion out his blessings as He
likes, nor favor anyone with his "grace". If a fellow creature
possesses a capacity which we do not possess, a fine quality
inciting our admiration and respect, we must not think that
he has received more; he has only availed himself better
than we have done of a simple power of his nature[14]. We are,
therefore, not to hope for anything from the God of the
Theosophists. He cannot "give" us anything. After all, our
life is not a "gift" of his. He has not even "willed" that we
should exist. Our existence is only a mere necessity, independent of the divine will and to a certain extent superior to it.
In the course of centuries, different forms of being emerge
from the eternal interior of God and appear on the screen of
Space and Time. The God of the Theosophists is indifferent
to all, He loves no one, He hates no one. He looks frigidly at
everything—he is a "God of Ice", and his stern look is similar to that of Ananke[15], Nemesis[16] or Karma.

But in that case, why say prayers to God? The lady-founder
of the Theosophic Society has foreseen all the logical consequences of such a Creed. And that is why she strongly objects to prayers composed of a certain number of words that
one repeats with the mouth . . . such as were inaugurated
by the Jews and popularized by the Pharisees[17]. Here is the
precept of the theosophists: "We act instead of talking"[18].

Although Annie Besant who, after the death of Mrs. Blavatsky, ruled the Theosophic Society during many years, de-
fends prayer against the "modern spirit", by showing that the
religious spirit is not possible without "prayer"[19], and that, at
least in certain cases, not all "efficacy" can be denied it, this
theosophic prayer has nothing in common (except the name)

with prayer that tradition and the history of religion has made us familiar with. It is only a kind of telepathic influence by means of which the will of the person who "prays" affects in a quite physical and, so to speak, mechanical way, the soul of another (a charitable person) suggesting to him the idea of helping the one who prays. Annie Besant illustrates her doctrine by the case of a certain George Muller of Bristol who died in 1898; every time that his orphanages were in financial difficulties, he addressed himself with confidence to God and his prayers were always granted: some charitable person would invariably send him the relief he needed[20].

It follows from what we said previously that so far as his salvation is concerned man cannot expect any outside help, any "assistance". For no one can help him. "Well and good", says Theosophy. It is just this conquest (salvation) that obtains the greatest happiness for us. What we obtain through our own efforts is worth more, in our opinion, than what we receive gratuitously[21]. It is, therefore, an excellent thing that man should be obliged to gain his salvation by his own efforts, using his own strength. For him salvation will no longer be a kind of "reward"; it will be his own triumph, his conquest. It is to him and not to another that belongs the glory of having "freed God."

3. "To free God", means to expel from one's soul all evil: sin, passions, unruly inclinations, inordinate tendencies, wrong propensities, bad habits, to establish in the soul order and harmony, to adorn it with all kinds of virtue; to make it resemble God; much more: to make it "equal" to God.

But is it possible to assume that man left to his own resources will be equal to a so great and so difficult task in the course of a single life? Will a single life, even if we suppose it to be a long one, be sufficient for the profound transformation which must take place to raise the human monad from the lowest grade of animalism up to the fulness of divine perfection, that is to say, to the consciousness of his identity with the Moral Ideal, with God? If the evolution of species requires—as the partisans of this theory believe—incommensurable periods of time, how long will the evolution of souls take from the initial epoch when the monad began to open up to moral life to the moment when it rejoins God? "One life, even if prolonged, is no more adequate to gain knowledge, acquire experience, solidify principle and form character, than would one day in infancy be adequate to prepare for the duties of mature manhood"[22]. "It is impossible to attain perfection" says A. Besant, "in one single life. With our vague ideas, our undisciplined emotions, our activities so frequently pervaded by egotism and avidity, we cannot attain divine perfection before leaving this life. . . ."[23].

This is the real reason for re-incarnation, which is the logical postulate of the whole theosophical system. And, it is no exaggeration when Theosophists affirm that the idea of re-incarnation is a "fundamental thesis" of Theosophy.[24]

Indeed, how could a man bereft of any "supernatural" help attain to his own perfection, of which the Theosophists speak, during the limited period of one life? His natural forces are so inadequate, his task is so tremendous: a man who, at the beginning, does not differ much from an animal, to change into an angel, into God!

[1] H. P Blavatsky, *The Key to Theosophy*, London, 1893, pp. 2, 42, 46; W. Q. Judge, *An Epitome of Theosophy*, 1922, p. 11.

[2] C. Jinarajadasa, *First Principles of Theosophy*, Adyar, 1922, pp. 78, 122, 123.

[3] William Q. Judge, *op. cit.*, pp. 12, 13. H. P. Blavatsky, *op. cit.*, p. 147.

[4] Annie Besant, *Popular lectures on Theosophy: What is Theosophy*, Chicago, 1910, p. 73.

[5] Annie Besant, *Evolution of Life and Form*, London, 1918, p. 15.

[6] Annie Besant, *A study in Karma*, Krotona, 1918, p. 39.

[7] Annie Besant, *Popular lectures on Theosophy: What is Theosophy*, Chicago, 1910, p. 6; *Evolution of Life and Form*, London, 1918, p. 15.

[8] C. Jinarajadasa, *Przeg. Teozof.*, Sept. 1925, pp. 25-26, C. Jinarajadasa, *The message of the Future*, Glasgow, 1916, p. 74.

[9] C. Jinarajadasa, *ibid.*, p. 31.

[10] C. Jinarajadasa, *op. cit.*, p. 25 See Annie Besant, *Esoteric Christianity*, London, 1901, p. 30 f.

[11] Annie Besant, *Evolution of Life and Form*, London, 1918, p. 15.

SALVATION

12 Cf. H. P. Blavatsky, *The Key to Theosophy*, sect. V. Point Loma, Calif., 1913, p. 63—Annie Besant, *A study in Karma*, Krotona, 1918, p. 6.

13 *L'âme et le corps d'après Spinoza*, Paris, Alcan, pp. 95-106. *Spinoza et le panthéisme religieux*, Paris, 1950, Book III.

14 Irving S. Cooper, *Re-incarnation, the hope of the world*, Krotona, p. 22.

15 H. P. Blavatsky, *The Key to Theosophy*, London, 1893, pp. 134, 135, 146.

16 H. P. Blavatsky, *The Sacred Doctrine*, Vol. I, London, 1888, p. 642; *The Key to Theosophy*, Point Loma, Cal., 1913, p. 206.

17 H. P. Blavatsky, *The Key to Theosophy*, London, 1893, p. 45.

18 *Ibid.* (ed. London, 1893), p. 45. See Jerome A. Anderson, *Karma*, San Francisco, Cal., 1896 p. 16.

19 *Esoteric Christianity* London, 1901, Chap X, p. 295.

20 *Esoteric Christianity*, N. Y., 1902, pp. 282-283.
"What has happened? His prayer was a strong, energetic desire, and that desire creates a form, of which it is the life and directing energy. That vibrating, living creature has but one idea that ensouls it: help is wanted, food is wanted; and it ranges the subtle world, seeking. A charitable man desires to give help to the needy, is looking for an opportunity to give. As the magnet to soft iron, so is such a person to the desire-form, and it is attracted to him. It rouses in his brain vibrations identical with its own—George Muller, his orphanage, its needs. . . . . Quite naturally George Muller would say that God put into the heart of such a one to give the needed help" (*ibid*, pp. 282-283). In reality, Mrs. Besant notes, "the result could be obtained equally well by a deliberate exercise of will, without any prayer, by a person who understood the mechanism concerned and the way to put it into motion" (*Ibid.*, p. 283).

But Mrs. Besant was quite conscious that this way of understanding the efficacy of prayer cannot explain all. Because, besides other reasons, the telepathic forces have their limits. It is for this reason that she appeals to the influences which play on the astral terrain. "Some one temporarily out of the physical body and at work in the invisible worlds, or a passing Angel, may hear the cry for help, and may then put the thought of sending the required aid into the brain of some charitable person" (*ibid.*, p. 285).

We find the same doctrine of the efficacy of prayer in other works of Mrs. Besant, notably in *The Ancient Wisdom*. "Many a mother's loving prayers hover round her son as angel-forms, turning aside from him evil influences that perchance his own thoughts are attracting" (*ibid.*, p. 64). "These prayers with their accompanying ceremonies are more or less useful according to the knowledge, the love, and the will-power by which they are ensouled. They rest on that universal truth of vibration by which the universe is built, modified and maintained. Vibrations are set up by the uttered sounds arranging astral matter into definite forms ensouled by the thought enshrined in the words" (*ibid.*, pp. 103-104). It is in this way, Mrs. Besant adds, that we can help our dead by our prayers. "These forms-thoughts are directed towards the kamalokik entity, and striking against the astral body hastens its disintegration" (*ibid.*, p. 104).

What is generally called "malefice" can be explained in a similar way. "An elemental ensouled by a malignant thought will hover round its victim seeking opportunity to injure him. But neither the one nor the other can make any impression unless there be in the astral body of the object something akin to themselves, something that can respond accordingly to their vibrations, and thus enable them to attach themselves. If there be nothing in him of matter cognate to their own, then by a law of their nature they rebound from him along the path they pursued in going to him—the magnetic trace they have left—and rush to their creator with a force proportionate to that of their projection" (*ibid.*, pp. 64-65). See also H. P. Blavatsky, *The Key to Theosophy*, London, 1893, p. 46-47.

21 Hubbe-Schleiden, *Karma a fondament of theosophical morals*, Szkice Teozof., Warszawa, 1912, p. 57.

22 Quoted by Jerome A. Anderson, *Re-incarnation a study of the human soul*, S. Francisco, 1896, p. 69. See also *ibid.*, pp. 68-69.

23 Annie Besant, *The Changing World*, Chicago, 1910, pp. 111-112, 191. See also Allan Kardec, *Le Ciel et l'enfer*, Paris, 1923, p. 23; F. Szumski, *Swiat Ducha*, June-July 1934, p. 15.

24 Annie Besant, *The Changing World, Chicago*, 1910 p. 111. Irving S. Cooper, *Re-incarnation the hope of the world*, Krotona, 1920, Introd.; A. Besant, *A study to Karma*, Krotona, 1918, p. 1-2.

CHAPTER II

MORAL SANCTION

1. If we wish to pass judgment on the moral value of the re-incarnationist doctrine, we must examine the sanction which this doctrine suggests for its precepts; since every moral system is based on a sanction.

The partisan of re-incarnation—at least if he is consistent —does not recognize eternal punishment[1]. According to him, all men without exception will, by means of the mechanism of successive re-incarnations, reach moral perfection, eternal happiness. "As evolution is always progressive"—we are told by Gustave Geley—"all beings without exception will escape from evil; all will reach happiness, but they will reach it more or less quickly, according as they more or less conform to the laws of evolution. . ."[2]. It is merely a "question of time". Therefore the Theosophist does not say to a man: "Wake up, you have only a single life before you; if you lose it, you will have lost all and forever", but only: "Do well what you do, for otherwise you will have to return to this earth to do again what you have not done well".

How weak is this sanction of re-incarnation! It reminds us of a philosopher who, anxious to possess a certain thing, is said to have exclaimed: "To have it, I would give 100,000 years of my future happiness"! And he would not have calculated too badly for one may indeed be willing to lose 100,000 years when one is sure of eternity.

2. And if it were only inefficacious! What is much worse is that it is eminently dangerous for the moral destiny of men; at least, of men as they usually are. It is dangerous because far from turning men away from evil passions, it stirs them up; the man addicted to his passions desires noth-

ing so much as the earthly life which alone gives him the possibility of indulging in them, and instead of working for his own amendment, he will plunge more and more into sin. Even the thought of death, which has deterred from Evil more than one sensual man, would become an encouragement to vice. They would say more than ever: "Comedamus et bibamus, cras moriemur" — let us enjoy life while it lasts. But beyond this life? Beyond, it will be a return to the same earthly life, to its enjoyments in a renewed body, more beautiful, full of youth and fresh forces. "For those who so pitifully cling to youth and the pleasures of the young, re-incarnation holds the promise of renewed youth, of life after life"[3].

Even the sentiment of honor which restrains so many bad propensities, loses much of its force in the hypothesis of reincarnation. For indeed, if a life of disorder brings dishonor to the Theosophist, he consoles himself with the thought that his punishment will be of brief duration; at the dawn of his next existence he, and all those who have known him, will have lost any recollection of it.

It is true that Theosophy teaches that sooner or later the sinner will hate his own moral misdeeds because of the pain they will inflict upon him, and that in the end he will mend his ways. "He will freely reject the things whose possession ultimately causes him pain; he will no longer desire them when he has experienced to the full that their possession ends in sorrow"[4]. But it is much more likely that this thought will harden him in his sins instead of restraining him. He will say to himself: let us make the most of this life while we are still far from this undesirable change.

The danger with which the re-incarnationist sanction menaces the moral life had already been mentioned by St. Cyril. "Is it really in order to punish the soul for its misdeeds, (he said ironically to the believers in re-incarnation), that you unite it again to the body? No doubt, you want to teach it by experience how vile passions are? Would it not be better to turn the eyes away from Evil than to plunge the soul deeply into the most abject pleasures? ... That is how you may save it". Have a healthy fear of acting as a bad physician who dispenses to the patient the very thing which does him the most harm![5]

In a celebrated dialogue Aeneas Gazaeus attributes to Axitheus these words: the partisans of re-incarnation act like a senseless judge who would sentence a thief, not to death, but to enter into a temple and steal there whatever he might want[6].

3. How strange! The objection we have just made to theosophical Morality, the Theosophists charge against Christian Morality. Here is what we read in the Theosophical Essays of the great adepts of hermetical Science: If a man really believes that we live only once, the conclusion that he cannot fail to draw from this assertion, namely that he should not impose any restraint on himself, would be quite logical.

The author of this remark (Hubbe-Schleiden) confuses the anti-re-incarnationist Morality with that which denies the existence of a life beyond the grave; for it is only when one admits the postulate of the latter morality that the argument of the author acquires any force.

4. If one wishes to estimate the weakness of the re-incarnationist sanction it will be sufficient to ask oneself this question: Who will ensure this sanction? Who is its real guardian? We know what they will answer. It is Karma.

But that does not satisfy us. What is Karma? We are told that it is a "law" in consequence of which justice is administered "unerring"[7] and "without prejudice": Karma causes every action, every word, even every thought, to be followed by an effect adequate and proportionate to it: a good effect follows a good action, a bad effect, a bad action[8].

But let us continue our enquiry. If Karma is able to estimate the moral value of human actions with such precision, should we not attribute to it wisdom greatly surpassing any human wisdom, an "intelligence" infinitely acute and from time to time reaching to such a point that it might be considered as a person possessing all these qualities to a degree which is called Infinity? Here the Theosophists appear especially embarrassed. They usually content themselves with quoting the words of the lady who founded their sect: "If you question me about the causative intelligence in it (Karma), I must answer you, I do not know"[9].

But this intelligence which penetrates the most secret thoughts of man, is it not "human consciousness" pure and simple? No, and for a very simple reason: namely that "human consciousness", if we are to believe Theosophy, is nothing more than "the sum total of the recollections of our past experiences". "Conscience is not the gift of God", Annie Besant says, "but the outcome of experience"[10]. In proportion as we gather the bitter fruit of our bad actions, of our wrong sentiments, of our guilty thoughts, (hence under the influence of Karma!), "consciousness is awakened in us"[11]. In other words, consciousness is not Karma, it is the effect of Karma! Thus Karma, in its inner essence, remains for us ignotum X[12].

5. But if the nature of Karma remains for us an eternal mystery, may we not know, at least, on what arguments belief in its existence is based?

In his primitive mentality, the Hindu does not ask himself this question; he "feels" justice diffused in the universe —and that suffices him. He "feels" that in the world the existence of justice is a necessity, and he does not enquire beyond that. For him, Karma is not a conclusion reached by arguments; it is rather the point from which the arguments about re-incarnation start. The law of Karma is known to him by immediate intuition and therefore requires no proofs. In this case, it is a question of psychic attitude, of "mentality" and not of construction founded on logic.

I owe a great part of my knowledge of this mentality to the kindness of my distinguished colleague, R. F. Matrubuta Isvara Balasubramaniam (Balam), a former professor at the Gregorian University in Rome. He is well informed on the question for he is of the caste of the Brahmins and professed faith in re-incarnation and in the law of Karma until the age of 23, when he received baptism before entering the Society of Jesus. When I asked him what were the "proofs" alleged by the Brahmins in favor of Karma, he answered, not without a shade of irony, "Proofs? My country-men do not need any! Besides", he added, "the idea of proof has not the same meaning in the Brahmin mentality as in the mentality of you Occidentals". And as an illustration of what he had just said: "Here is the classical thesis invoked by us to show that all religions are equally good, that all of them lead to God: one may reach the summit of a mountain by following different paths; the rivers fall into the same ocean; we may reach God equally well by following the way of one religion as of another". It never occurs to the mind of a Hindu to try to substantiate in any way the analogy which they hastily invoke between mountain paths and rivers on the one hand, and religion on the other. They do not see that as long as they do not justify such an equalisation, they are simply making a comparison, they are only playing with a metaphor. Such is their mentality.

Theosophists are quite aware that they will never be able to convince Occidentals by this kind of argument. And that is why they look for "proofs", and "positive" proofs, founded on experience. Such are the proofs which the Occidental mind prefers to all others. It is "the experience of thousands of ages"—so Mrs. Blavatsky assures us—"that has shown us the existence of absolute and unerring equity, wisdom and intelligence"[13].

Is that quite true? Is it quite true that, without having first established the existence of God, the supreme Judge of Good and Evil, one can ever prove, by experience alone, "absolute and unerring equity, wisdom, and intelligence" with reference to the dominion of supreme justice in this world? Certainly not. For in that case, their conception of

re-incarnation would be deprived of its principal support. Indeed, one of the main beams of the re-incarnationist building is (and this is admitted by the re-incarnationists themselves) the ascertaining of the sad fact that one single life
would not be sufficient to justify the assertion of Salomon,
"that he had never seen the righteous forsaken, nor his seed
begging their bread"[14]. Very often Nature seems to betray
some "partiality" in allotting her gifts and thus commits more
than one "injustice".

Hence, the "justice of Karma" which to every action, even
to the most insignificant, would attach a sanction infallibly
wise and strictly proportioned to the misdeed, is not an "experimental fact"! It is rather a kind of extension into the
moral world of the physical law of "action and reaction"[15].
And so true is this that when it is a question of proving the
justice of Karma, almost all authors appeal to this physical
law: every action in Nature provokes infallibly a reaction
equal to the action [16]. But by what right do we submit to
such a generalisation? How can this extrapolation of a
mechanical principle into the moral sphere be justified?
One may look in vain for a reply.

The "sanction of Karma" has no logical foundation. It is
a blind faith in the bad sense of the term. It is a "bias".

6. We are, therefore, no longer astonished to see it exposed
to controversies within the very School whose faith it should
support, and these controversies bring discredit to the mind
of whoever is endowed with critical sense. To illustrate
what has just been said, we shall give a concrete example:
a child is born in ideal conditions; he is from a rich, honest,
healthy, esteemed family; he receives a good education, he
behaves well during his youth and wins all hearts. The
partisan of the justice of Karma will say: This is the reward of a virtuous life led by him in a previous incarnation.
But now it happens that one day a catastrophe befalls this individual; he catches a horrible and incurable disease, or he
is the victim of an undeserved disgrace. It is the punish-

ment of misdeeds committed during another previous incarnation, the believers in the idea of Karma will say.

Then was the Karma of his birth nothing but an illusion? asks the learned Hindu, Pahumunay[17]. Or are we to suppose that Karma may suspend its sentences? The latter hypothesis would not correspond to the character of the physical law which they attribute to Karma. For, just as fire cannot suspend its effects and must burn at once all that is near to it, so Karma cannot delay the execution of its justice[18]. Mrs. Blavatsky tries to solve this difficulty by saying that only the initiated (seers and great adepts) can know the characteristics of Karma[19]. Now what is the value of such an affirmation? It would be difficult to see in it anything but an avowal of ignoramus et ignorabimus. The great lady-founder of Theosophy does not herself know the mysteries of Karma!

Mrs. Besant refers here to "the Lords of Karma". We are told that they are "the great spiritual intelligences who keep the karmic records and adjust the complicated working of karmic law"[20]. They are said to be identical with "Lipikas" (who keep a register of Karma) and with "Maharajas" (the agents of Karma on earth), of whom Mrs. Blavatsky speaks. The Lords of Karma, Mrs. Besant says, have the duty of "superintending the working out of causes continually set going by thoughts, desires, and actions"[21]. This theory only puts our difficulty one step further back. For it is necessary to prove first the existence of these lords; in the second place, it must be demonstrated how they can know all that concerns the life of human beings, in particular their inmost thoughts and wishes; finally, by what kind of activity they direct the Karma, considered by the Theosophists as the "supreme law" to which all else is subjected? Decidedly, the belief in "Lords of Karma", borrowed from the Sages of the Orient, only complicates the difficult problem of Karma.

THE ENIGMA OF THE HEREAFTER

1 "The endless hell . . . being only a nightmare dream of ignorance, hate, and fear" (Annie Besant, *The ancient wisdom*, Adyar, 1939, pp. 83-84).

2 *L'être subconscient*, Paris, 1911, pp. 154-155.

3 Jerome A. Anderson, *Re-incarnation a study of the human soul*, S. Francisco, 1896, p. 181.

4 Annie Besant, *The ancient wisdom*, Adyar, 1939, p. 200.

5 *In Joannis Evangelium*, I, 6; P. G. 73, 135.

6 Θεόφραστος. P. G. 85, 894-895.

7 ". . . this mysterious, inexorable, but, in the equity and wisdom of its decrees, infallible law. . . ." (H. P. Blavatsky, *The Key to Theosophy*, Point Loma, 1913, p 139); "unerring Law of Retribution" (H. P. Blavatsky, *The Secret Doctrine*, Los Angeles, 1925, Vol. 1 p. 634). Cf. Annie Besant, *A Study in Karma*, Krotona, 1918, p. 2.

8 "But we believe firmly in what we call the *Law of Retribution*, and in the absolute justice and wisdom guiding this Law of Karma" (H. P. Blavatsky, *The Key to Theosophy*, Point Loma, 1913, p. 108). "We believe in an unerring law of Retribution, called *Karma*, which asserts itself in a natural concatenation of causes and their unavoidable results" (H P Blavatsky, *ibid.*, p. 139). Cf. Annie Besant, *A study on Karma*, Krotona, 1918, p. 1.

9 *The Key to Theosophy*, Los Angeles, 1920, p. 157.

10 Annie Besant, *Popular lectures on theosophy; Re-incarnation, its necessity*, Chicago, 1910, p. 36. See Irving S. Cooper, *Re-incarnation the hope of the world*, Krotona, 1930.

11 J. Ch. Chatterji, *La philosophie ésotérique de l'Inde*, Bruxelles, 1898, p. 78.

12 ". . . itself unknowable" (H. P. Blavatsky, *The Key to Theosophy*, London, 1893, p. 136).

This explains a great part of the striking inconsistency of theosophical terminology on this point. Karma is called either "the Lords of the Universe, (C. Chatterji, *Philosophie ésotérique de l'Inde*), or the "expression of the divine nature" (A. Besant, *Karma, ed. cit.*, p. 13), or man's "product" (A. P. Sinnett).

When the Theosophists speak of Karma, one may say that they only comment on the teaching of the Sages of the Orient.

It is also to the wisdom of the Orient that Theosophists owe their cult of the number Seven. The astral plan ("Kameloka") is composed of seven habitations (*The ancient wisdom*, ed. cit., pp. 90-101); the mental plan is divided into seven parts (*ibid.* pp. 107-131); the Heaven ("Devachan") also contains seven distinct divisions (*ibid.*, pp. 142-151); the progress of Humanity is accomplished in seven stages.

13 H. P. Blavatsky, *The Key to Theosophy*, Point Loma, Cal., 1913, p. 195.

14 Anderson, *op. cit.*, p. 179.

15 Annie Besant, *Popular lectures on theosophy, Re-incarnation: its necessity*, Chicago, 1910, p. 48.

16 See Annie Besant, *The ancient wisdom*, Adyar, 1939, p. 229. C. Jinarajadasa, *First Principles of Theosophy*, Adyar, 1923, p. 64.

17 J. Pahumunay, *The Buddhistic and Catholic Position*, Colombo, p. 45 (cf. Giov. Busnelli, S. J. *op. cit.*, p. 360).

18 This law exists "in the nature of things" (Annie Besant, *A study in Karma*, Krotona, 1918, pp. 3-4, 7, 11). "Karma being a natural law" (Annie Besant, *Karma once more*, Rochester, 1910, p. 6). "Karma is no more sacred

than any other natural law" (A. Besant, *A study in Karma*, Krotona, 1918, p. 5.

[19] H. P. Blavatsky, *The Key to Theosophy*, London, 1893, p. 135, 145, 146. Nevertheless Annie Besant believes that the "ripe Karma . . . can be sketched out in a horoscope cast by a competent astrologer" (*The ancient wisdom, ed. cit.*, p. 241). For there is a question of inevitable actions. "In all this, Mrs. Besant says, the man has no power of choice" (*ibid.*, p. 241).

[20] *The Ancient Wisdom, ed. cit.*, p. 246. "The Lords of Karma" "those angels of God's Plan whose work it is to adjust the good and evil of man's past and present. . . ." (C. Jinarajadasa, *First Principles of Theosophy*, Adyar, 1922, pp. 53, 57, 59, 68, 72, 74, 75).

[21] *The Ancient Wisdom*, Adyar, 1939, p. 192.

Chapter III

MORALS, AN INTEGRAL PART OF PHYSICS

1. In order to thoroughly understand the mechanism of the moral sanction of Karma it is most important to discover the exact meaning of the words "good" and "evil" in the Theosophic system. "Good", Mrs. Blavatsky says, "is that which promotes the development of life; evil is that which harms it"[1]. Mrs. Besant notes: "The right is that which helps . . . forward the progress of the soul. . . The wrong is that which retards evolution"[2].

But the extent of this development, according to the Theosophists, differs widely in conformity with individual souls; there are "old" souls, that is to say, souls that for many centuries have gone through the cycle of their successive re-incarnations, and there are also "young" souls that have only recently begun their purifying re-incarnations[3]. What is beneficial for some may not be so for others. Should we therefore think that "good" and "evil" have merely relative value and may be compared, for instance, to those foods which according to whether they are intended for a full grown and vigorous organism or for a young and weak one may be qualified as "good" or "bad"? That is exact, reply the Theosophists; moral "good" and "evil" have purely relative values[4].

This is how H. Hausbrandt summarises the doctrine of Mrs. Blavatsky on this question. Let us compare evolution to a ladder which a man must ascend. Let us consider three consecutive rungs. Each one of them supports a man. For the man who is on the third rung to descend to the second would mean retrogression, and, thus, to commit a bad action, an immoral act; for the man who stands on the first rung to rise to the level of the second would be, on the contrary, a good action, a moral act[5]. Therefore, although "conscience" prescribes to everyone what is good and what is bad ... it does not prescribe the same thing to everyone[6], the reason being that the moral law which is binding on us depends at every moment on the level our soul has reached[7].

2. This "moral relativism" which is a characteristic of Theosophy and assimilates moral goodness and badness to the utility or the harmfulness of certain actions with regard to our individual development, has nothing that should surprise us; it follows naturally and logically from the pantheistic principles on which Theosophy is founded. Indeed, in pantheism there is no room for "sin" (in the strict sense of the word) seeing that there is no room for "Divine Right". "To sin" is simply "not to know the end to which our efforts should tend if we are to promote our own welfare"; sin is simply a "mistake"[8]. And that is why he whom society abhors as a "criminal" will not cease being a God[9]. Indeed, what are generally called "sins" are the actions that society (whose evolution is higher than that of the "sinner") defines as "bad"[10]. "The negation of the existence of Evil in the human heart is one of the noblest ideas of Theosophy"[11].

This conception of sin clearly shows how moral values are classified in the Theosophic system by means of knowledge. But this knowledge of "good" and "evil" cannot be either an a priori knowledge or an analytic knowledge, seeing that they presuppose the existence of norms of fixed value, of general, unconditional and immutable rules. Now, no evolutionist[12] can admit the existence of such rules. The knowledge meant here cannot be anything other than an a posteriori knowledge, a kind of experience: we must ascertain what is good and what is evil at each stage of our development by means of our own faculties alone; for "if somebody tells us that a certain action is bad, we may refrain from doing it for a certain time, but we are fundamentally not quite convinced of the truth of what we have been told[13].

3. But here is the disastrous consequence of this way of looking at things: since the only means of teaching us to re-

cognize Evil is experience of Evil, it must be permissible (at least at some period of our evolution) to commit evil deeds.

This paradoxical conclusion offends in the highest degree our moral sense, but it forces itself on the Theosophists. In the great school of this world, they say, they want to teach us to be good while respecting our liberty and so we are allowed to do Evil. There is no other way to make us know it[14]; to know it we must be convinced that the law exists and we cannot learn this unless we persist in satisfying our desire to get possession of all that we covet. Thus it is that by means of a real experience, either pleasant or painful, we may judge whether or not the pleasure was in harmony with the law[15].

But if we are allowed to do Evil has anyone the right to punish us for our bad actions? Theosophy, yielding again to evidence, also admits this second conclusion. Indeed no one, so it teaches, "punishes" us for our sins. God does not punish us, for He is not "our Lawgiver" (we have already drawn attention to this idea when referring to the God of Theosophy), "Karma" does not punish us either; for in general, as the Theosophists teach us, "Karma" neither punishes nor rewards us[16]. What we call "punishment" of a "bad action" is merely a physical "consequence" of our activity and nothing more[17].

Hence, we see that, after all, Theosophy reduces the moral problem to Ontology, morality becomes an integral part of Physics. "The astral body", Mrs. Besant says, "is constantly changing its material under this play of the passions, appetites, desires and emotions. All good ones strengthen the finer parts of the body, shake some of the coarser constituents, draw into it the subtler materials, and attract round elementals of a beneficial kind that aid in the renovating process"[18]. "All evil ones have diametrically opposite effects, strengthening the coarser, expelling the finer, drawing in more of the former, and attracting elementals who help in the deteriorating process"[19]. "Purification proceeds along the same

lines as in the former case—the expulsion of lower constituents by setting up vibrations antagonistic to them, and
the drawing in of finer material in their place"[20].

4. This Ontologism of a new kind would result in serious
consequences for everyday life. Let us suppose that a man
has committed a crime; he is taken to the Court of Justice and
is sentenced. What right have you to punish me, the man
might object. By committing what you are pleased to call a
"crime", I have simply acted under the impulse of my
"Dharma" which, according to our teaching, is nothing else
but the intimate nature of a creature, the level it reaches at
a certain moment of its evolution; besides, this "Dharma"
is a Moral law which has compulsory force for the creature
at the moment and which conditions all its ulterior evolution.
You know full well that the moral law depends strictly on
the degree of evolution which I had reached at the time when
I committed that action; that an imperfect life in agreement
with our own Dharma is better than a perfect life regulated by
the Dharma of another. Do you not also say that the Dharma
of a savage is to gratify all his cravings? Did you yourself
act differently when you were still a primitive man, a savage?
You admit that you were then still "dominated by your passions ... those of a murderer ... that you felt hatred and
anger"[21]. If now you surpass me from the moral point of
view, "if you have more spiritual strength", it is only because your evolution commenced sooner than mine[22]. When
I have gone through as many re-incarnations as you have, my
Dharma will be very different from that which I possess at
present; it will be exactly like your own Dharma of today.
And then I too will no longer commit crimes! Patience! It
is merely a question of time[23]. Besides, are my actions really
useless? Do they not give others the opportunity of paying
their Karma? The guilty man would thus silence his judges.
And, if, in spite of his protestations, they were to persist in
punishing him, one would certainly accuse them of being
unjust and cruel.

THE ENIGMA OF THE HEREAFTER

[1] Hedvige Hausbrandt, *Przegl. Teozof.*, Sept. 1925, p. 35.

[2] Annie Besant, *The Ancient Wisdom*, ed. cit., pp. 186-187; See also C. Jinarajadasa, *First Principles of Theosophy*, Adyar, 1923, p. 63.

[3] Annie Besant, *Popular lectures on Theosophy, Reincarnation: its necessity*, Chicago, 1910, p. 46. See also Irving S. Cooper, *Reincarnation the hope of the world, Krotona*, 1920, pp. 11, 15, 38.

[4] See F. e. J. C. Chatterji, *La philosophie ésotérique de l'Inde*, Bruxelles, 1898, pp. 84, 100. C. Jinarajadasa, *First Principles of Theosophy*, Adyar, 1922, pp. 46-47.

[5] Hedvige Hausbrandt, *l. c.*, p. 36.

[6] See *Szkice Teozof.*, p. 53.

[7] H. Hausbrandt, *l. c.*, p. 32.

[8] F. C. Jinarajadasa, *Przegl. Teozof.*, May-August, 1922, p. 28.

[9] Annie Besant, *Popular lectures on Theosophy*: III *Reincarnation its necessity, Chicago*, 1910, p. 46. See *ibid*. IV *Reincarnation: its answers to life's problems*, Chicago, 1910, p. 49. C. Jinarajadasa *l. c.*, p. 29.

[10] *Przegl. Teozof.*, Sept. 1925, p. 37.

[11] C. Jinarajadasa, l. c., p. 29.

[12] Theosophy admits evolution!

[13] C. Jinarajadasa, *l. c.*, p. 27.

[14] A. Besant, *The ancient wisdom*, Adyar, 1939, p. 18 f.

[15] *Ibid.*

[16] Jerome A. Anderson, *Reincarnation, a study of the human soul*, S. Francisco, 1896, p. 181: "The Divine law of cause and effect which neither punishes nor rewards, but wisely, justly, and inexorably adjusts each cause to each corresponding effect. . . ."—See A. Besant, *A Study in Karma*, Krotona, 1918, p. 9.

[17] See Annie Besant, *op. cit.*, p. 10: "A natural law is a sequence of conditions; such a condition being present, such another condition will invariably follow".

[18] *The ancient wisdom*, ed. cit., p. 6.

[19] *Ibid.*

[20] *Ibid.*

[21] *Przegl. Teoz.*, Oc. Nov. 1921, p. 18.

[22] See *Przegl. Teoz.*, Dec. 1921, pp. 30-31; Sept. 1925, p. 32.

[23] Annie Besant, *Popular lectures on Theosophy, Re-incarnation: its necessity*, Chicago, 1910, p. 49.

Chapter IV

MORAL PROGRESS

1. By the light of "Moral Physicism", which we have just explained, it is easy enough to understand how, according to the doctrine of re-incarnation, a development in the moral life, moral progress can be achieved.

Our whole life, Theosophy teaches, is a chain of causes and results; each cause gives birth to a result; the result becomes in its turn a cause; and so on. Consequently our moral life is nothing more than an uninterrupted chain of "moral causes and their results", our actions are so many "energies" which, projected by us, reflect themselves on those external objects at which we have aimed; they then come back to us as moral incitements resulting in new actions which in their turn call forth new reactions—and so on indefinitely[1].

2. But does this way of looking at things authorize us to speak of moral "progress"? The idea of "progress" seems to be inseparable from that of personal initiative, of an initiative which is meant to break at will the monotonous chain of actions and reactions governed by the mechanical laws of equivalence. It depends on the inventive spirit, the creative genius which imparts a new and original order to material things; which, so to speak, changes their course and directs them towards achievements they could never have reached through the work of their own forces alone.

True "progress" is inconceivable in a system based on the physical axiom that "action is equal to reaction". A machine which only gives back in a different form the energy supplied by us does not "progress"!

Now, if we are to believe the doctrine of the Theosophists, man is nothing but a machine, a spiritual machine! His moral development is merely an "exchange of cosmic energy". The monad, Mrs. Besant explains, contains all the possibilities of all imaginable vibrations. This is why any vibration which reaches the monad produces in it a counter-vibration of the same kind. In this way all energies of the monad pass successively from the latent to the active state[2], "from the potential to the kinetic state, as a physicist would express it", adds another Theosophist[3]. Here lies the secret of evolution, Mrs. Besant concludes[4].

And it is truly a "secret". "Evolution" always presupposes the production of something not yet existent. But, in this case, nothing new is produced. One sees only a kind of deploying of realities preexistent in the human monad. All the divine powers and forces—says Mrs. Besant—exist in this world, but only in a latent state, inactive, concealed... They must be gradually aroused by "external impacts"[5]. "As we gradually progress", insists another eminent re-incarnationist, "we add absolutely nothing to our own being, we only wake up whatever was already dormant within us"[6].

3. Such is the "evolution" of the spirit in the theory of re-incarnation! According to this theory, man is a spectator rather than an actor in the working out of his own perfection. He remains without initiative, originality, personal action. His ascent towards moral heights is then without beauty or glory. He might be compared to some motionless stone which cosmic forces would work upon by way of sudden "pains". He, whether he liked it or not, would be driven towards his destiny by inexorable laws, just as the plant which from an acorn becomes an oak. He could not possibly escape the forces that secretly move him, far less could he hasten their action. He would always have to follow the inflexible rhythm of the laws of Physics and his steps would be riveted to those of "necessity". Is not such a man a real automaton?

4. To reach perfection, this automaton must pass successively through all possible phases of human hope—say the Theosophists—and resist all forms of temptation[7]. But, in order to conform to this process, will he not have to go through

an infinite multitude of experiences, an infinite series of transmigrations? For in this way only could the human monad "pass through all possible phases of hope", "resist all forms of temptation", "tread all the paths of error"! Now, if one assumes that it has to pass successively through an infinite multitude of situations and go through an infinite series of transmigrations, it follows that it will never be able to reach perfection[8]. To be only an eternal pilgrim of the spiritual world, a kind of "wandering Jew" of moral evolution without any real result—such is the outlook offered to Man by the Theosophists.

[1] H. P. Blavatsky, *The Key to Theosophy*, London, 1893, pp. 138-139.
[2] *The ancient wisdom*, Adyar, 1939, pp. 171 156, 174, 176, 177, 260.
[3] *Ibid.* p. 171.
[4] *Ibid.*, p. 171.
[5] *Ibid.*, p. 171.
[6] Irving S. Cooper, *op. cit.*, p. 22.
[7] Annie Besant, *The ancient wisdom*, Adyar, 1939, p. 201.
[8] As science knows no limit, but progresses continually, to arrive at all possible knowledge by integration of particular knowledge, it is necessary to pass through an infinite multitude of possible situations and for an infinitely long time. Now, infinite time as well as infinite space are creations of the imagination and not real concepts.

Chapter V

THE STAFF OF LIFE

1. It is only the Ethics based on re-incarnation—so the re-incarnationists assert—that can bring the longed-for harmony, peace, tranquillity and happiness to the human heart, for it is the only entirely satisfactory solution to the eternal problem of Suffering and Evil[1] For this reason, it is the only true "staff of life"!

Indeed, how simple and clear is the solution of the problem of Evil that it offers us! If you are poor, sick, persecuted, slandered, saddened, in anguish, even in despair, or tortured by remorse, remember that all this is a punishment for having taken undue advantage of the privileges you possessed in a former life; or for the wrong that you inflicted on other people, for the tears that they shed on your account. But, take courage: if you patiently endure the sufferings which are your lot now, your Karma will soon change: as soon as your soul, after death, returns to this earth and enters again into a body, you will become rich, famous, strong, and handsome, in brief, happy! As happy as any of those you are envying now, who are only reaping the reward of their good deeds in a former life.

2. In order to appreciate to what extent these claims of the believers in re-incarnation may be justified, let us first consider a most important fact: a man stricken by any misfortune must always, if one clings to the ideology of re-incarnation, remember that whatever suffering he has to endure is a "punishment"[2].

However, a question immediately rises in his mind: a punishment for having done what? He knows absolutely nothing about it! At this point, common sense rebels: if I am "punish-

ed", I should at least know why. Here is the argument of
Eneas Gazaeus, a disciple of the neo-platonist, Hierocles:
"When I have to punish my son or my servant for any offense,
I first lecture him ('praemoneo') so that he may in the
future clearly remember the reason why he has been punished, and thus take good care not to relapse into the same fault.
When God sends us the most terrible punishments, should
He not enlighten those who have to suffer them as to the
reason for the same? Should He wipe out every remembrance
of our crime? . . . What benefit can a man derive from punishment if his fault is not pointed out to him? Indeed such
punishment defeats its own end, it irritates, it breeds revolt"[3].

One cannot but admit the justice of this old philosopher's
words. Not only should the man punished know in a general
way that he must have committed some fault, but know exactly
what it was. The other way of inflicting pain is unworthy of
man, of his reasonable nature; it really too much resembles
the way in which animals are trained! It is even inferior to
this "training". For, when one wants to train an animal, one
connects as far as possible the inflicted punishment with
the fault committed by the animal; one tries to make a kind
of synthesis between the suffering inflicted and the fault
committed.

On the other hand, our argument cannot be weakened by
recalling that the suffering inflicted by Karma has not the
character of a real "punishment", but that it is a simply
physical consequence of the act in question. For neither has
the suffering to which we submit animals the character of a
real "punishment". "Punishment" presupposes "a moral
fault", of which no creature devoid of judgment can be declared guilty. However, when we beat an animal, we are trying to make him associate the pain he feels with the act we
want him not to repeat; we try to combine in a kind of re-
presentative synthesis the pain and the mistake. Beating an
animal without having tried in some way to point out why is
sheer cruelty.

3. But our opponents will not admit they are defeated. They go on arguing: then a criminal could not be punished if he had forgotten the nature of his crime? It would be sufficient to cause anyone to forget his crime—by means of hypnosis, for instance—to relieve him of any responsibility[4]! Our opponent does not, as he should, discriminate between the two kinds of punishment: (1) the poena vindicativa, which aims at reestablishing a disturbed order, as required by the common welfare, and this by means of an exemplary expiation of the crime committed; (2) the poena medicinalis, the main object of which is to correct the one who errs. Whatever one may think of the first kind of punishment, it is certain that application of the second kind presupposes in a culprit the knowledge of his fault[5]. The re-incarnationist system, which on the one hand recognizes only the poena medicinalis and, on the other hand, denies to the culprit the knowledge or remembrance of the fault for which he is being punished, is illogical and incoherent.

4. In order to minimize the value of our objection, the advocates of re-incarnation point to the considerable value of forgetfulness of the crimes we committed during our former existences: we should be discouraged, they say, by the memory of them, and this discouragement would make the fulfilling of our actual duties more difficult: "If any one wants to drive his carriage well, he must devote all his attention to the road and to the horses; he must not look hither and thither. . ."[6].

This comparison is not a very good one. We realize at once that it would not in any way benefit the driver to "look hither and thither", to "admire the sights along the road or to compare any street with another. . ."[7]. Moreover, such a way of driving would be positively harmful. If the driver's attention is drifting, he is diverted from what he must do, hic et nunc; he himself, and other people are exposed to great dangers.

But matters are quite different in the case with which we

are concerned. In the course of every new incarnation, man must correct all that he did wrong in a past life. He must draw from the sight of the "consequences" of that life which are bad, a positive lesson, showing what it was worth from a moral point of view. This is why, when "punishment" for the mistakes of his former life is inflicted on him, in order to make him realize that they were "bad", he should, at the same time, be granted the memory of those faults and thus allowed to profit by the lesson.

The way in which certain other advocates of re-incarnation try to justify forgetfulness of our former lives is also far from satisfactory. Our ignorance about our former lives, they say[8], is a real blessing to us; for children and adolescents this memory would be disastrous and for all of us it would be a dangerous opportunity to fall into moral evil. This memory, adds Innoc. Calderone, would stamp our whole existence with a character of unbearable monotony; it would make it impossible for us to enjoy the freshness of life. It would be then the finality of oblivion that would serve to justify it.

But we must frankly recognize that this justification is very weak. It would seriously impair the conception of finality that exists in this world. For, if man cannot lead a dignified life unless he believes it to be his first, unless be believes that he is beginning an entirely new, perfectly fresh life, it means that at the basis of this world there is complete disorder, a real contradiction: human life would only be possible when supported by a lie, and ethics, which condemns lying, would be founded on a lie.

As to the risk of the memory of our former lives endangering our moral behavior, it is improbable except for children. For adults, this memory should rather be a help to them. Man, it seems, would look at his failures in the light of the "result" inflicted upon him. It would serve him a solemn reminder at each of his failings. But it would be precisely the contrary if one accepts the re-incarnationist viewpoint, for, according to this theory, children (as we have seen before) are the ones who best remember the details of their past lives, while the memories of adults are supposed to be weaker!

5. What we have said up to this point shows clearly that, contrary to what its partisans contend, the theory of re-incarnation is unable to supply us with "the solution of the problem of Suffering and Evil". Moreover, it makes this problem especially acute, for it considers any suffering, any Evil, as the natural consequence of a certain fault: redde, quod debes[9]. The theory of re-incarnation ignores the comforting words of Christ about the man born blind: "Neither has this man sinned, nor his parents; but that the works of God should be made manifest in him"[10]. It does not recognize "Suffering—a gift of God", as a gift of His infinite Love[11]. If Suffering is sent to man unaccompanied by Divine Love, it will also be borne without love. It will be an odious Necessity; it will appear as a cruel Vengeance, the feature of Nemesis.

This depressing view of Suffering in the theory of re-incarnation is also evident in the following: nothing could ever free man from moral suffering, since the redeeming expiation would be forever excluded[12], and repentance deprived of any "purifying" virtue[13]. The only way of wiping out one's faults would then be to suffer, to suffer all the consequences to the bitter end; to exhaust all the effects when they have reached their plenitude[14]. Would any resort be left against such a terrible fate? None. The only way out would be to patiently bide the time until the consequences of the fault have reached their full development. "It would be impossible either to delay or to hasten the Karma in the fulfilment of justice", the founder of the Theosophic Association expressly says[15].

If you have committed a fault (perhaps without any bad intention)[16], you will have to atone for it at the appointed hour and to all its consequences. You could not count on any help. In fact, according to the theosophic doctrine, any help is inadmissible, ineffective, and even harmful to a certain extent. And this is why: suppose a sinner on the way to accomplish his Karma happens to have to suffer the consequences of one of his faults. If, in your desire to help him, you free him from a special suffering, you do nothing but delay his expiation; you hinder the fulfilment of his moral evolution. Sooner or later, he will still have to follow his Karma to the end.

6. Some Theosophists are perfectly aware of this difficulty. Often, even in the Theosophic Association, Mrs. Besant points out, "I heard some members say: I cannot help this man, since what he is suffering is his Karma". It is like saying: I cannot pick up this child who just fell, since the law of gravitation is opposed to it[17].

Does this remark help us to solve the difficulty? Does it, for instance, show us how we could help a sufferer without delaying the fulfilment of his Karma? When it is a question of a child having fallen to the ground, I understand perfectly that I am really helping him by picking him up. This is because I do not believe that his Karma requires him to stay on the ground for a prescribed, definite time. I do not even consider his fall as "punishment" inflicted by his Karma; I only look on it as an accident! But those who believe that his Karma requires him to stay on the ground during a strictly determined time, think that picking him up wouldn't help him in any way; it would only interrupt the course of his expiation and postpone the fulfilment of his Karma. The child will again fall to the ground because Karma is "the law of Nature"[18], and "a natural law cannot be broken"[19]. He will remain on the ground until the time required by the Karma has elapsed.

To be sure, the ordinary man does not know whether the child's Karma requires him to remain on the ground a longer time than would reasonably be needed to bring him help. But —let us notice—this charitable action has for justification only the fact that we are absolutely ignorant as to the child's real Karma. Whoever thoroughly understands the mysteries of Karma will never perform any act of charity.

Fortunately, for the generality of mankind this ignorance of the Karma excuses the act of charity, always commendable[20], and in this respect Mrs. Besant's opponents were quite wrong. But, nevertheless, it remains true that, according to the theosophic theory, the act of charity is devoid of any rational foundation; which suffices to reveal the fundamental incoherence of the system.

7. But here is an even more serious aspect of the question. What the re-incarnationists call "help to life" is, in some cases, capable of driving a person to one of those tragic acts inspired by despair. Let us suppose a man has committed an involuntary murder. The re-incarnationists will tell him that he must atone for it[21]. Some of them (the Occultists in particular), drawing their inspiration from Plotinism, will even describe with many details, the future atonement: the murderer will be reborn to be murdered in his turn[22]; the son who killed his mother by mishap, will come back to earth to be killed himself by one of his children[23]. Nothing could ever free him from this horrible menace! No one will ever pronounce words of forgiveness for him, he will never hear the formula of absolution which would give him back some courage[24]. May not this terrible thought induce him to seek his own punishment, to precipitate his own fate? Alas! the history of mankind records many suicides due to such a motive[25].

Such is the "help" offered by "re-incarnation" Ethics!

---

[1] "The doctrine of palingenesy offers a wonderful explanation of evil" (Gustave Geley, *L'être subconscient*, Paris, 1911, p. 153).

[2] "Karma", J. H. Connelly says, "rewards merit as unerringly as it punishes demerit" (See Jerome A. Anderson, *Re-incarnation a study of the human soul*, S. Francisco, 1895, p. 174).

[3] P. G., t. 85, col. 902.

[4] Jerome A. Anderson, *Re-incarnation a study of the human soul*, 1896, p. 164.

[5] See Saint Irenaeus, *Contra Haeres.* lib. II, c. 33; P. G. 7, 830, 831.

[6] W. Lutoslawski, *Niems. duszy*, p. 288; *Preesistenza e Rincarnazione*, Milano, 1913, ed. cit., pp. 62-63; K. O. Schmidt, *Die Wiederverkörp. der Seele*, p. 39.

[7] W. Lutoslawski, *Preesist. e. Rincarn.*, ed. cit. p. 63.

THE STAFF OF LIFE

8 *La Rincarnazione, inchiesta internazionale*, Milano, 1913, p. 23, Cf. Busnelli, S. J., *La Rincarnazione*, II ed., 1925 pp. 285-286, Irving S. Cooper, *Reincarnation the hope of the world*, Krotona 1920, p. 74.

9 Man "must inevitably suffer the effects of the causes which he himself originates" (Jerome A. Anderson, *Karma*, San Francisco, Cal., 1896, p. 92). "No wrong we inflict can escape final punishment" (Jerome A. Anderson, *Reincarnation a study of the human soul*, S. Francisco, 1896, p. 175).

10 *St. John*, IX, 3.

11 I have spoken of this at length in my public lectures made in Rio de Janeiro and at Fordham University; *The Philosophy of Evil*, New York, 1951.

12 Jerome A. Anderson, *Karma*, San Francisco, Calif., 1896, Chap. XII, pp. 101-107. The exclusion of the intermediary Redeemer is the logical consequence of the refusal of "grace". See H. P. Blavatsky, *The Key to Theosophy*, London, 1893, p. 150.

13 H. P. Blavatsky, *op. cit.* pp. 135, 146. Jerome A. Anderson, *Karma*, San Francisco, Cal., 1896, Chap. XII p. 108-112.

14 H. P. Blavatsky, *op. cit.*, pp. 134-135. William Q. Judge, *The Ocean of Theosophy*, Los Angeles, 1915, p. 95: ". . . none can escape either by prayer, or favor or . . . any other intermediary".

15 H. P. Blavatsky, *op. cit.*, p. 137.

16 Sin, according to theosophy, is simply "ignorance", as we have already said. It does not necessarily imply an "evil will". Mrs. Besant says: Let us suppose that a newborn child dies almost immediately after birth. "The explanation from the standpoint of re-incarnation is that in the past . . . such an Ego had become indebted to the law of causing the death of someone, but without malice, without intention, killing by some passing carelessness or folly"; e.g., "a man threw a match when he lighted a cigar, without seeing, if it were out, and it fell upon a heap of straw which blazed up and set fire to a cottage, and a person was burned to death" (Annie Besant, *Popular lectures on theosophy, Re-incarnation: its answers*, ed. cit., pp. 51-52).

17 *Przegl. Teozof.* N. 6, May-August, 1922, p. 8. See also J. C. Chatterji, *La philosophie ésotérique de l'Inde*, Bruxelles, 1898, pp. 99-100.

18 Annie Besant, *Popular lectures on theosophy: V: The law of Action and Reaction*, Chicago, 1910, p. 67.

19 *Ibid.*, p. 67.

20 *Ibid.*, p. 80, See pp. 81-82.

21 See above note 76.

22 It has been truly observed that justice as the theory of re-incarnation states it is the leveling of one injustice by another. *A* has been murdered by *B*, *B* will, in his turn, be murdered by *C*. The latter will have to die by the hand of *D*. And so on in infinitum.

23 *Enneades*, III, II, 13 (ed. Brehier, Paris, 1925, p. 40 ff).

24 "The Karma works. There is no escape. There is no such thing in nature as forgiveness" (Annie Besant, *Popular lectures on theosophy, V: The law of Action and Reaction*, Chicago, 1910, p. 82). "All such forgiveness of sins (as we read of in the Gospels) may be termed declaratory; the Karma is exhausted and a 'knower of Karma' declares the fact" (*Esoteric Christianity*, N.Y., 1902, p. 309). See also Jerome A. Anderson, *Re-incarnation a study of the human soul*, Fourth edition, S. Francisco, Cal. 1896, pp. 170-174.

25 René Guenon, *L'erreur spirite*, Paris, 1923, pp. 236-237.

CHAPTER VI

JUSTICE

1- Re-incarnation alone, its partisans claim, gives us the clue to "injustice", that injustice which shocks us at every step[1]. The idea of re-incarnation explains why we are unequal from a physical point of view, an intellectual point of view, a moral point of view, a spiritual point of view; why some enjoy a healthy and strong body, while other have a weak and sickly one; why some possess culture and personal charm, while others only have a homely, and sometimes repulsive, appearance; why the intelligence of some people is keen and alert, and that of others is dull and slow; finally, why exterior circumstances create so many revolting inequalities and seem to indicate a kind of favoritism[2]. Gustave Geley says in the work already mentioned: "We are only what we have made ourselves, through our own efforts, in our successive lives; thus unconsciously preparing, in each re-incarnation for the following one; actually enjoying the progress already accomplished; making use of those aptitudes that we have developed; and, in the same way, suffering from those bad tendencies that we have allowed to take possession of us"[3]. Thus we owe whatever we are to our own personal merits, and this is the unavoidable consequence of Karma. Whoever is thoroughly imbued with these ideas will never think of complaining about his "destiny" and will no longer consider it as a harsh stepmother. He will no longer envy his neighbor's lot[4].

And the partisans of re-incarnation point out that: if the proletariat now rebels against social inequalities, if they allow themselves to be dragged into political agitation, this is only because they ignore the doctrine of Karma. They have not yet grasped the fact that the existing "inequalities" coming from such deep roots cannot be uprooted by means of a simple decree issued overnight[5]. They do not yet understand that the improvement of the social standing of any individual depends on the improvement of his Karma and consequently of his life: his acts, his words, his thoughts.[6] "The social consequences of the scientific conception of palingenesy," says Gustave Geley, "are no less important. When men are sure of their indefinite evolution in successive lives and under very diverse circumstances, then they will reconcile themselves to the natural and temporary inequalities, which cannot but result from the law of evolution[7]".

2. In order to fully appreciate all these affirmations, let us see if we may not have conceived a wrong idea of "justice". Unfortunately, this is only too true. The concept of justice has been mistaken for that of equality.

What is justice? It is the virtue that tends to make us render to everyone his due. Believers in re-incarnation admit, as we do, this conception of justice. But how can we proceed from these premises to the conclusion: participation in the goods of life must be the same for everyone, so that the least inequality in this distribution would be a real "injustice"? The answer is clear: by exalting man to the height of God, as does Pantheism, or by lowering God to the level of man, as does Naturalism.

In truth, as God owes nothing to a "grace" or "gift", but possesses all by virtue of "necessity" inherent to His nature, if one admits Pantheism (which, so to speak, identifies man with God)[8] one gives to man an unlimited, absolute right to all that his natural capacity allows him to possess. The limits of his capacity would be the limits of his rights. Spinoza who enunciates this conclusion in pathetic words has very clearly grasped the logic of his system, which is definitely pantheist. We have discussed this in another work. On the other hand, if we adopt the concept of Naturalism, we lower Divinity to the level of man. God becomes a kind of President of a Republic and the distribution of all goods is regulated by the laws of the Republic and the will of Parliament. If He does not submit to these laws, He commits an injustice. As soon as one admits that man receives nothing from God but by virtue of "justice", it is easy to demonstrate that each man has the same right to worldly goods; that each man's lot must be equal to his neighbor's. For such a right would belong to each individual by virtue of his very "nature". But human "nature" is the same in all men!

3. From all that precedes, it follows that the reproach of injustice made by the disciples of re-incarnation to the God of Christians is fundamentally unjust[9]. In reality, the God of Christians is not the God of the pantheists: nor is He merely a President of a Republic. He is an almighty Lord, the absolute Master of the Universe, of which He is also the Creator. Whatever He grants to me has inevitably the character of a "gift". Now, a "gift" is not a thing which has definite form and is immutable like a geometrical figure, nor is it the result of a mathematical "necessity"; it is the fruit of love: of love, the creative and inexhaustible original force.

The gifts we bestow on our loved ones as tokens of our affection, vary a great deal according to the feeling of our hearts. When a re-incarnationist contemplates offering a present, he does not fail to remember his friend's wishes. Consequently his gifts vary a great deal. So far as he himself is concerned he has never thought of adopting a uniform and definite type of present which would answer every purpose. Would it not be absolutely unjust to apply to God a rule which would be absurd in our own life? Moreover, would it not be foolish to have such a wish? We have nothing to gain by wishing that the infinite multiplicity of the manifestations of God's love be reduced to any uniform expression!

In order that the perfectly just "gift" be the same for all, the beneficiaries should first be absolutely identical. So the reproach of the re-incarnationists implies perfect equality. But perfect equality means stagnation, the end of life; it means death. For it implies the end of the human species. In fact, the wish for only one species of living beings in this world, presupposes the disappearance of all specific differences. Then the universal fight between the species, emphasized by Darwin, the dramatic aspect of which Mrs. Besant stresses, would be brought to an end. What would then become of living beings, all equal, all "brothers", compelled to continue to exist on the surface of a planet where they would be the only inhabitants, and from which all plants and all animal species would have vanished at the same time? In order to live they would have to devour each other. An attractive ideal of justice, indeed, which would force these fraternal philosophers to partake of such a "meal together"!

4. Frightened by the consequences of their assertion, the disciples of re-incarnation will perhaps reply: we do not want to abolish the differences between the species; we only want to do away with individual differences. We desire that all men be equal, absolutely and in every way; or, at least, that it may be so when they have reached the end of their physical and moral evolution, when their souls will have, so to speak, reached their majority.

Eminent critics of the theory of re-incarnation (René Guenon, for instance) remark at this point that the postulate of absolute individual "equality" includes an intrinsic contradiction: does not setting aside individual differences mean the setting aside of the individualities themselves? Two individuals equal in every respect cannot be differentiated, they become identical; they "coincide" (as Leibnitz said); they have no difference but one unique reality, from which duality is excluded [10].

But we will forego this argument which seems rather weak. In truth, two corporal beings, even supposed to be perfectly identical, could always be differentiated by their matter, which must (always) connect them in a different way to Space. Thomism and Kantism agree on this point. Two individuals, even if exactly alike, will nevertheless represent two different individualities.

We prefer to make another objection to the disciples of re-incarnation: on what is the postulate of individual "equality" based? Certainly not on experience, for (and the disciples of re-incarnation admit it formally) this emphasizes at each step shocking "inequalities" in the moral as well as the material sphere. It is not based on an a priori judgment. We saw this before when we showed that the absolute equality of all creatures could not be inferred from the idea of God nor from the idea of creature.

Thus, the postulate of absolute equality is a sheer presumption. It was invented (history proves this) by Socialism and then passed on to Theosophy through Spiritualism. We know, in fact, that Mrs. Blavatsky before founding the Theosophist Association, practiced Spiritualism under the influence of Allan Kardec, the founder of French Spiritualism, and of his friend Michal, who worked at developing in her (Mrs. Blavatsky) the faculties of a medium[11]. They inoculated her with the virus of "absolute equality" for which they were indebted to the French Socialists[12].

5. The explanations just given show to what extent the reproach of "injustice" sometimes aimed at the God of Christians is in itself unjust. We shall be still more conscious of this fact, if we scrutinize the form in which some re-incarnationists present the objection. "Let us do a little thinking", they say, "a wretch who has had to face all kinds of difficulties without finding a way out, and has managed to get through only by crime, happens to die; or let us say, an idiot dies, who for lack of knowledge had lived a life of sin. Neither of them possessed the criterium of good and evil; neither, to tell the truth, knew what he was doing. However, as they die in a state of sin, they will both suffer eternal punishment"[13]. This objection implies belief in the theosophic conception of sin. For the Theosophists, sin is merely a physical violation of law, whether it be voluntary

or not! And retribution is no more than the physical result fatally following any given action. The objection fails to stand when one accepts the idea of sin as taught by Christian doctrine, according to which sin is deliberate transgression of God's law. An idiot is, by definition, unable to "deliberate" before acting and consequently unable to "sin".

6. One more point has to be examined: the social question. Is it true that the doctrine of re-incarnation offers the best solution? We do not intend to deny that this doctrine may offer a fairly satisfactory solution of the social problem to those people who have lived for many generations in a re-incarnationist atmosphere. But we doubt very much that this solution will satisfy other people, especially those who have, for many centuries, breathed the pure air of Christian teaching about the equality and fraternity of all men in Jesus Christ. In fact, the re-incarnationist solution presupposes the existence of a hierarchy of "castes", or at least, it would logically result in such a social organization[14]. Whoever has committed a sin during one of his successive lives will have to atone for it in another. The proof, the infallible proof, we are told, that he really committed this sin, is precisely that he was born in an unfortunate condition[15]. Now, as this very condition is nothing else but his Karma, he must not try to free himself from it! It would mean wasting his labor: he has no choice, but must accept his present state and live according to the rules forced on his "caste"!

Those who no longer profess faith in Christ will not welcome the solution of the social problem proposed by the re-incarnationists. Their proud and selfish souls will not easily be convinced of guilt regarding those "terrible faults" with which their conscience does not reproach them. They will not be soothed by the beautiful promise of a compensatory re-incarnation in a more or less distant future.

"Envy", the breeder of social revolutions, will not be eliminated by the re-incarnationists, because it is based on pride. Now do not the partisans of re-incarnation encourage this pride; do they not exalt it by extolling to their disciples, the principle of "self-sufficiency" and, consequently, the futility of prayer, of grace, etc.; by teaching them that all that they possess—qualities, virtues, properties, positions, honors and even the least important advantages of which they boast—is their own work, the result of their own efforts, the reward of their own merits[16]?

7. On the whole, the only idea that is worth remembering in connection with the solution of the "social problem" advocated by the disciples of re-incarnation is the following: the real increase of the material welfare of humanity is only possible insofar as the spirituality of Man increases. The root of those unhealthy symptoms, social diseases, lies too deep to be reached by means of legislative measures or other police regulations.

But this idea is not a discovery of the re-incarnationist gentlemen! It is the very essence of what the Church, inspired by Christ, has been teaching humanity for twenty centuries.

[1] Jerome A. Anderson, *Re-incarnation, a study of the human soul*, S. Francisco, 1896, p. 179.

[2] Annie Besant, *The necessity of Re-incarnation*, London, 1905, pp. 16-20. "Why are some people born deformed, dwarfs and cripples? That is the result of cruelties inflicted upon others, paid for by deformities in another birth..." (A Besant, *Popular lectures on theosophy; Re-incarnation: its answers to life's problems*, Chicago, 1910, p. 57). Irving S. Cooper, *Re-incarnation the hope of the world*, Krotona, 1920, p. 15.

[3] *Op. cit.*, p. 155.

[4] H. P. Blavatsky, *op. cit.*, pp. 145, 151.

[5] Jerome A. Anderson, *Re-incarnation*, fourth edition, S. Francisco, Cal. 1896, p. 179.

[6] Ibid., pp. 179-180.

[7] *Op. cit.*, pp. 156-157.

[8] "The universe . . . is one whole. This whole is what is denominated Deity by Western Philosophers" (William Q. Judge, *An epitome of theosophy*, Los Angeles, 1922, p. 9-10). See also A. Besant, *Popular lectures on theosophy: What is theosophy*, Chicago, 1910, pp. 6, 7. A. Besant, *A study in Karma*, Krotona, Cal., 1918, p. 6. A. Besant, *Why I became a theosophist*, New York, p. 6.

[9] E. g. Jerome A. Anderson, *Re-incarnation*, fourth edition, San Francisco, Cal., 1896, p. 168--175.

[10] See *L'erreur spirite* Paris, 1923, pp. 203-204.

[11] René Guenon, *Théosophisme*, Paris, 1921, p. 11.

[12] René Guenon, *L'erreur spirite.* Paris, 1923. pp. 200-201.

[13] Wolowski, *Antropozofja Rudolfa Steinera.* Warszawa, 1925, p. 32.

[14] Cf. Th. Henri Martin, *La vie future suivant la Foi et la Raison,* Paris, 1870, pp. 417-422.

[15] Irv. S. Cooper, *op. cit.,* chap. I and II.

[16] See Jerome A. Anderson, *Re-incarnation,* fourth edition, San Francisco, 1896, pp. 180-181. Annie Besant, *Popular lectures on theosophy, Re-incarnation: its necessity,* Chicago, 1910, p. 37: "Every virtue you have, you have built during your life of bliss in heaven . . . You are the master of your future character and therfore of your destiny".

CONCLUSION

1. It cannot be denied that the re-incarnationist belief has, in spite of its intrinsic weakness, progressed rather rapidly in the course of the last decades. How can such a success be explained? By "the mentality of the times", without having to look further. One knows, in fact, how favorably contemporary *scientists* welcome "the law of conservation of energy", the "law of closed causality" and the "law of evolution". These three laws represent "the spirit of the times", the mentality of this period, in modern science. Now the re-incarnationist theory, understood as scientific synthesis, is based on those three laws, and its fervent advocates not only admit it but derive some pride from this fact[1].

In the *religious* sphere, "the spirit of the time" is the negation of transcendentalism, that is to say: immanence. And the theory of re-incarnation, as already demonstrated, necessarily implies immanence. Wishing to conciliate re-incarnation with the idea of God's transcendence, is trying to marry Karma with Grace, an endeavor which can profit neither the Karma nor Grace. For, striving to limit the dogma of the Karma so as to make it fit into the frame of the definitions of Grace would amount to pretending to make of necessity a free thing, or of free will a necessary thing. If some re-incarnationists sometimes unite these two concepts, it is only because they have not perceived the consequences of such confusion.

In the *social* sphere, "the spirit of the time" is the mirage of "absolute equality" for everyone. Now the re-incarnationist theory, as has been pointed out several times, claims the principle of "absolute equality" as the foundation of its system. After this mould, it shapes its particular idea of justice, an idea which pretends to assign limits to God's power and make Him a kind of President of a republic.

CONCLUSION

2. It is this "spirit of the time" which, in our opinion, chiefly contributes to spreading among the masses, especially among the lower middle class, the idea of re-incarnation.

Will the future be as propitious to this doctrine as its advocates proclaim? We doubt it. For the "spirit of the time" is only the spirit of a single period of time, that of our passing epoch.

Very few people today venture to declare that the "law of conservation of energy" (suggested by some experiments with matter) can be applied to the activities of the mind[2]. The "law of closed causality" formerly admitted by Wundt, Riehl, Paulsen and many others, is more and more considered as an unverified hypothesis, and moreover, as a hypothesis to which experience is opposed, an arbitrary hypothesis; in one word, a simple "prejudice". Finally, the "principle of evolution", as the evolutionists themselves admit, loses ground day by day; it is entering a period of "crisis"[3]. Moreover this principle concerns the species, and not the individual. It is the species which according to it develops ad infinitum. The individual has just enough time to transmit his acquired attributes to posterity, then he disappears forever.

The spirit of dreaming, of the pursuit of fancies, which took pleasure in roaming among the stars[4] is now replaced by realism, a rather rough realism, we must admit. The new generation, as pointed out by educators, shows, day by day, less liking for fantastic imaginings.

At the same time, Naturalism, a logical consequence of the negation of divine transcendence, follows a similar movement of regression[5]. The countless miseries and sorrows following the catastrophe of 1914 and that of 1939 caused many afflicted people to lose their confidence in Naturalism. They look for a refuge and another hope in a superior Supernatural order; that of religion.

Pantheism remains. But Pantheism is not inseparable from the thesis of re-incarnation; Spinoza and several German philosophers, builders of cosmogonies, reject the idea of re-incarnation. Moreover, if one considers the violent fluctuations of contemporary thought, more than one symptom seems to indicate that the end of the golden age of Pantheism is very near.

1 Annie Besant, *The necessity of Re-incarnation*, London, 1905, pp. 8, 9, 11.
2 This problem is the principal object of our book *La Psychophysique humaine d'aprés Aristote*, Paris, 1930.
3 This problem was examined in our *Psychologia Metaphysica*, Romae, 1948, pp. 469-501. See *Transformismo Antropologico*, Sao Paulo, 1945.
4 See W. Lutoslawski, *Preesistenza e Rincarnazione, ed. cit.*, pp. 149-151. Irv. S. Cooper, *Reincarnation the hope of the world*, Krotona, 1920, p. 43-46.
5 The aims of human beings as conceived by theosophy shock us by their materialism. This is evident in Irv. S. Cooper's books which have great authority among Theosophists. The Christian's heaven does not please the author. Why? Because it excludes temptations, scientific and artistic problems, political questions as well as economic, social, industrial, national, international ones; books, newspapers, travels, sciences, and inventions.

INDEX